Foreword

Symeon N

Doncaster, or Danum as it was named by the Roman settlers, was chosen as a northern outpost because of its geographical location. Being central in England and situated right in the centre of the main trading routes it was the perfect setting both for trade and defence. Although the Romans were responsible for the early success of Doncaster it had been an important settling place since the Iron Age. The archaeology of the region proves that fact and it has been said by learned men that if the archaeology of Doncaster were celebrated as much as York celebrates its, then Doncaster would be the better of the two.

From a life-long love of local history this book has been born. It is generic in nature and covers a multitude of subjects. Many books have been written to inform the populace of events from the past and most of these books have one thing in common. They deal with a particular theme and are limited by the constraints that themes bring. I have overturned this notion and written freely about everything and anything that has this town as its common denominator. Therefore, this book covers the history of Doncaster from prehistoric times to the modern day. It revisits time honoured theories and encourages you, the reader, to look upon the facts from a different perspective; after all, history is a science where we might have many theories, none of which is any truer than the other.

Until the time machine is invented we will never know for sure. All this said I will attempt to sail as close to the facts as possible within these pages.

Chapter 1

Prehistoric Doncaster

When the Romans arrived on our shores records began to be kept and many people mistakenly believe that this was the beginning of our town. If you thought that you would be wrong.

When we talk about prehistoric Doncaster we are referring to an era between 10,000 BC and AD 43 which is quite a long time period. Progress was slow and laborious. Homo sapiens inhabited our land for tens of thousands of years and modern humans, those like me and you arrived in Britain at least 25,000 years ago, that's before the last ice-age even started. In fact, it was this ice-age, moving north to south that beat them back into Southern Europe. Our landscape then was a desolate, barren and lifeless one pretty much uninhabitable. Because most of the earth's water was turned to ice the sea levels were around 417 feet lower than they are today. This meant that one could wander from England to both Ireland and Europe without getting ones feet wet! The retreat of the ice sheets and the warming of the climate led to settlers returning to our area about 10,000 BC. Palaeolithic (Old Stone Age) hunter gatherers used caves and natural outcrops for shelter and as bases for hunting. To aid them with this, they produced tools, blades and axes from a readily available material, namely flint, and a number of these tools have been discovered in the Doncaster area over the years. A single flint blade was discovered in the centre of Doncaster during an excavation at St Sepulchre Gate in 1976, this piece has been dated to the late upper Palaeolithic period, circa 10,000 – 7,500 BC. In addition to this, other similar finds have been unearthed at Rossington, Bawtry and Hatfield Woodhouse.

The next, more recent era, is the Mesolithic (or middle stone-age) period, circa 7,500 – 4,000 BC. During this period the landscape is beginning to repair itself. It is being transformed from a treeless icy landscape to a more wooded one, this, in turn, increased the potential for human habitation as plant and animal sources grew stronger. Mesolithic groups would have made good use of this transition, following grazing animals during the warmer months and moving to coastal hunting grounds as winter set in. The fact that these settlers led such a nomadic lifestyle means the evidence of their presence is sometimes a little hard to find, that said, there is evidence of a camp/settlement in the Don Gorge between Sprotbrough and Conisborough.

The New Stone-age (Neolithic) period, 4,400 – 2,500 BC, was characterised by the introduction of farming and a synthetic changing of the landscape, by this I mean 'Long Barrows'. These are large burial mounds, two of which have been discovered and identified at Sprotbrough and Melton Warren at the west side of Doncaster. Although evidence of this period is extremely scarce in South Yorkshire, Doncaster has found other sites with a concentration of Neolithic flint tools.

Flint tools were great and in many ways essential for the lifestyle back then, but technology advances and new and better ways of doing things are sought. Introducing, the Bronze-age. Circa 2,500 – 800 BC.

The Bronze-age saw the introduction of copper and bronze working, which is great news for the modern archaeologist as extremely well preserved metal axe and spearheads have been found around Doncaster. Although this was a revolution of its time, manufacture of these implements was a highly skilled trade and so not everyone had the knowledge, or indeed the ability to create them. This is evidenced by a find from St Sepulchre Gate where a bronze age flint dagger was uncovered, illustrating the fact that older tools were still very much in use during a time when better technologies were available. Just because Ferrari's are available doesn't mean I am in a position to trade in my Toyota! The way we cared for the deceased was evolving too, we were moving away from burials and towards the cremation of remains. Thanks to this change a number of cremation urns have been discovered in Doncaster helping to build a better picture of our ancestors then. It has been speculated that the natural terrace of ground to the south of the river Don would have provided a suitable site for a cemetery at this time. The first discovery of this type of cremation came in the shape of an urn unearthed from a sandpit in Dockin Hill in 1844, it contained a small cup and an axe head, and similar finds have been discovered in St Sepulchre Gate and French Gate.

Finally we arrive at the Iron-age, 800 BC – 43 AD. At this time South Yorkshire as a whole fell victim to extensive farming like it had never known before. The advent of aerial photography proves this fact very well. From the air we can clearly see the extensive areas of fields and settlements, defined by ditches, enclosures and trackways. The underlying disturbances cause the crops and vegetation to behave differently with bare soil showing different colour shades. We can confidently date these forms to that of the Iron-age by analysing their shapes and comparing them to other, similar archaeological excavations. We can also date these by looking at the terrain and what is happening below ground. Overlying evidence, i.e. a Roman road might cut across a rectangular enclosure thus identifying it as pre-Roman.

By the late Iron-age, Doncaster was in a pretty strategic position geographically, lying right on the border between the tribal groupings of the Brigantes to the north and the Corieltauvi to the south, in fact it is likely that the boundary line was the River Don. There was a ford across the Don very near the present site of Doncaster at this time making the crossing point an extremely important place for both tribes. All that said, when it comes to evidence of Iron-age habitation of Doncaster, there is surprisingly very little, the two main discoveries are the town ditch and a section of wattle fence that were unearthed during excavations on the north side of Hall Gate during 2003.

Bog bodies.

A man was found in Thorne moors lying at his length with his head upon his arm, as in a common posture of sleep, whose skin being tanned, as it were, with the moor-water, preserved his shape entirely. About sixty years ago, or seventy, the servants of 'Mr. James Empson, of Goole, was digging turf in this great Waste, and one of them cut a man's arm off by the shoulder, which he carried home to his master, who took the bone out and stuffed it, and made a present of it to Dr. Johnson of York, an antiquarian. This was the very hand and arm mentioned by Dr. Gibson, late bishop of London in his Translation of Camden's Britannia, in the additions to the West Riding of Yorkshire. And in June 1747, in the neighbouring moors, and 'on the said Levil, in the moors belonging to Amcotts, was found by John Tate of Amcotts, who was digging turf, the entire body of a woman. He first cut of one of her feet with his spade, on which was a sandal; but frightened he left it. I being informed of it, went with Thomas Fect, my gardener, and others, and we took up the whole body; there was a sandal on the other foot ; the skin was like a piece of tanned leather, and it stretched like a fine doe skin; the hair was fresh about the head and privy parts, which distinguished the sex; the teeth firm; the bones were black; the flesh consumed; and she lay upon her side in a bending posture, with her head and toes almost together, which looked as though she had been hurled down by the force of some strong current of water; and though a great part of this moor had been formerly graved off she lay seven foot deep from the present surface. I took the skin of one arm, from the elbow to the hand, and shaking the bones out, it would have made a ladies' muff. The other hand not being cut with the spade, as we dug for it, I preserved it, and stuffed it, first taking out the bones, which my son, James Stovin, now has in his possession, at Doncaster. And what is very remarkable, the nails are firm and fast on the fingers. He also has one of the sandals, which was made of one whole piece of a raw hide, and only one short seam at the heel, sowed with a thong of the same leather. The sandals had ten loops cut in the whole leather on each side, and ten small loops at the toe, which caused the toe of the sandal to draw up like the mouth of a purse. They were laced on, upon the top of the foot, with a thong of the same leather. This lady's skin and the sandals were both tanned by the black water, for there being such great quantities of oak, firs, and other wood hurried in these moors, the water is by them tinctured and made exactly of the colour of the modern tan fat water, and the fir having so much resinous matter in it, no doubt that helps to preserve these bodies for so many ages, for that they have laid some hundreds of years'.

I have the assent of that learned body, the Royal Society, for in September 1747, I sent the hand and sandal above mentioned to that learned body with the same account (or to the same purpose I have here given), and when they returned it, I was honoured with their thanks by letter, and their opinion was that they must have laid there many hundred years; for the sandals were worn in England about the conquest, yet they could not find they were of the make or shape of this above mentioned, but concluded it must be much more ancient than that period. I buried the remains of this lady in Amcots chapel yard, I showed the hand and sandal to my worthy friend Thomas Whichcot, of Harpswell, esq. Knight of the shire for the county of Lincoln in parliament, who was pleased to put the sandal on before I sent them to the Royal Society.

At Thorne, in these moors, about ten years ago, as one William Biddy, of Thorne, was digging turf, he found the entire body of a man with his teeth firm in his head ; the hair of his head firm and fast on, and of a yellowish colour, either naturally so or dyed by the water of this moor. His skin was like a piece of tanned leather. He took the body up entire, after having lain there some hundreds of years. N.B.-I had this account from the man himself. I also think: proper to mention that the servants of Mr. George Healey, of Burringham, on the east side Trent, and near this Levil, was digging tip firewood in a large moor belonging to Burringham, and at the bottom of a fir tree root they found (as though laid together) a British spear, a British axe, and two short swords or dirks, all of brass, which Mr. Healey made a present off, and which I now have by me.

 Among the many objects that came to rest in the wet bog-lands, there are some that provide exceptionally detailed information about the past. This is because they were deliberately deposited directly into water under circumstances that assured their survival. The best examples of this phenomenon are the bog bodies. Bogs can be treacherous places and it is likely that some of the bodies found in the peat were those of travellers who slipped into bog pools and were trapped. Some ancient bodies found in the peat were supposedly found clutching heather or sticks as if attempting to haul themselves out. Other bodies found in bogs are deliberate burials. In Germany the bodies of a man, woman and child were found in a bog. They were fully clothed and laid upon animal hides, with bunches of flowers placed upon the bodies. In Northern Ireland a woman's body was discovered in Drumkeeragh Bog in Co. Down in 1780. She was dressed in a woollen costume. Fragments of the clothing are in the National Museum. Sometimes strangers who died in rural communities in the Middle-ages were buried in unconsecrated ground, and so were women who died in childbirth.

Many bog bodies have been found in Denmark and Britain, some a few thousand years old. Many of these bodies were never examined in detail and most were reburied without study or were badly damaged.

Chapter 2

Roman Doncaster

There is ample evidence to establish the fact of Roman occupation of Doncaster, but at what period of time it became a military station is uncertain. It was a station (Danum) on the direct line from Eboracum (York) to Lindum (Lincoln), and on account of its natural features and geographical position must have been one of great importance. According to the Notitia Dignitalum, the official directory and army list of the Roman Empire, 'the perfect of the Crispian horse under the Dux Britannia garrisoned there'. In ancient as in modern warfare, the food supply of the army had to be secured, and the possibilities of being unexpectedly attacked by a lurking foe guarded against. The consideration of these questions probably led to the selection of Danum as a camp for the Crispian Horsemen. To estimate, if only approximately, the importance of Doncaster as a military station, and the gigantic task of subduing a brave and resolute people, we must first inform ourselves concerning the geography of the district under consideration.

The Don rises to the west of Penistone, and by a devious course passes Penistone on its way to Sheffield. Its several tributaries, which rise on mountain moorland, desolate wastes, and places of wild and inspiring grandeur, join it by the way.

Five rivers like the fingers of a hand, fling from black mountains, mingle and are gone. Where sweetest valleys quit the wild and grand, and eldest forests o'er the sylvan Don, bid their immortal brother journey on, a stately pilgrim watched by all the hills.

From Penistone to Sheffield it flows from North to South, but at the latter place it entirely changes its course, taking with it the waters of the Rother and also a few miles further on, the waters of the Dearne. Although the district through which it passes from Sheffield to Doncaster is not overhung with such high hills and the outline thereof is not so rugged as those above Sheffield, yet it is diversified, beautiful, and teeming with historic interest. After passing Conisborough, the change of scenery is great, geologists tell us that here is a plateau four or five miles in width and extending from North to South across the river basin, a beautiful stretch of fertile land. The river passes through this plateau and at Hexthorpe enters a level plain which extends to the Humber. Scarcely a vestige of the former condition of this vast plain now remains, and in places there is nothing whatever on the surface to indicate the waters of the Don once flowed that way. This is owing to the draining of Hatfield Chase by Vermuyden, which took place in 1626. Before reaching Doncaster, the Don cast off an arm which after travelling a short distance was reunited to the main stream. A part of the town now stands on the island thus formed, but the relative positions of the island and the Roman camp cannot now be determined. Nearing Fishlake it again divided as also it did when it was near to Thorne, here it took a northerly direction and taking along with it the waters of the Went joined the Aire at a point near to the ancient town of Snaith. The two arms took an easterly bend, and meeting, became one. This stream received the united water of the Torne and the Idle, and taking a northerly course joined the Trent near to the junction of that river with the Ouse. The condition in past ages of this level country through which the ever threatening Don wormed its way nearly baffles description. In the main it consisted of river islands, water-logged islets, extensive moorlands and boggy wastes, forests and forest swamps. In some places there was a vast network of mere's, streams, pools and dykes, formed in beds of peat between 1 and 20 feet thick.

Even from this somewhat meagre description of the district immediately surrounding Doncaster it will be seen that the Roman camp, Danum, was on the edge of a land 'flowing with milk and honey', and facing a district, a natural stronghold from which the hunted Briton could successfully make periodical incursions into the cultivated parts.

Abraham de la Pryme, the historian of Hatfield Chase and adjacent parts draws a quaint and striking word picture of how this was done, and how the Romans, almost despairing of getting rid of so persistent a foe, were driven to try different methods to obtain their object. He says, "Sometimes one party had the victory and sometimes the other, but fortune generally fell to the Brigantes,

'who issued out of ye Wings of ye Wood, which stretched on both sides ye Champain, oftentimes hedg'd ye Romans in and cut them off or else decoyed them into abuscades, where they could destroy them at pleasure'.

The Romans regarded this forest as greater than,

'Ye strongest Citty in ye Wold unto them'

and determined to destroy it by fire. Fire and the axe did their work but the Briton was unconquered still and returned again and 'made ye reliques of this wood fastnesses, and places of safety, and began to annoy the Romans by their excursions almost as much as ever'.

As a last resort, the whole countryside was flooded by the Romans where which 'drave all ye Brigante's and other Malecontent Brittons out of ye same, drounded a great many number of them and turned the reliques of ye whole forest into a great lake and ye weight of ye waters so deprest ye soil of ye country lying for a good way on ye west of ye breach that it is lower than the rest unto this day'. De la Pryme was a fellow of the Royal Society, and obtained considerable distinction as a natural philosopher. If his description of the work of the Romans in flooding out the Britons be correct, a more desolate scene could not well be imagined. Letting in the waters of the estuary of the Humber would certainly submerge part of the country in question, but as certainly never drive out of the other parts, the stubborn native, whose riddance the Romans were so anxious to secure.

Probably the marshy parts already described in conjunction with the action of the Don presented far greater obstacles in the way of the Roman commanders than those offered by the forests. There was a similar tract of wild moor where the Don and its tributaries take their rise. No doubt it was across this waste, the conqueror marched from York to Chester in 1070. "The horses of the Knights were swallowed up by the treacherous swamps and swept away by the torrents". A similar fate would await the Roman horseman if he dared to venture where the extensive peat beds of Thorne and Goole moors now yield annually, thousands of tons of valuable litter. Human agency has so completely altered the conditions under which the water passes down the Don valley that there is no danger to the lowland from flood.

It was not so always, think of those times when the Don was in an angry mood, after a protracted frost or during a sudden storm, the waters gathering at a height of nearly 2000 feet above the sea level would rush through gorge and valley with irresistible force, gathering in bulk and power as it passed along, ploughing through the plateau, and with a final rush, spend its energies in working desolation and change on the woody and marshy plain where dwelt the unconquered Briton.

With the exception of the remains of an ancient forest of large trees, some of them cut down and squared by the axe, others cut down and prepared as if for fencing and other purposes, together with broken axes, wedges, and similar implements, scarcely any evidence of the occupation of this marshy district has been discovered. The number of human remains, manufactured articles, and coins etc, brought to light is indeed small. Some remains have been found at Austerfield, written Oustrefeld in Domesday, where tradition says a great battle was fought between the Romans and the British Tribes. Osterius is said to have commanded the Roman legions on that occasion, and that his name and the place of battle still survive in the village named Austerfield. The reason for mentioning this place is that it was probably the site of a Roman camp. Until recently evidences of a camp could be met with and Roman remains could be found in the locality. The nearness of this camp to the marshy plain warrants the assumption that its soldiers took an active part in the difficult task referred to above.

Whether the camp at Danum was formed before or after the subjugation of the native tribes is a question which need not be too closely inquired into. The date of its construction in no way affects the importance of its position. It was probable that the conquered people were placed under restraint, but whether in native villages or in some sort of military camp is a question not easily answered. They would have to work and were probably compelled to grow corn for the army, assist in making roads, draining the swamps and follow other useful employment. At the time of this writing there is nothing to help us to form an opinion of the political life of Roman Danum, outside the military organisation we cannot say whether it was only a village, or it held a higher position in the scale of municipal organisation. Probably its rank was that of a stipendiary town; being on the direct line between two important Roman colonies many distinguished Romans may have spent a night there, if not longer, but no evidence has survived to warrant us in assuming that in any period of its history it was the home of a thriving colony of cultivated and wealthy Roman citizens.

But, hark, the tramp of the Roman legions is again heard in the land. The Crispian horse along with the vast army of occupation turned their faces Rome-ward, finally leaving the shores of Britain, never, never more to return.

Chapter 3

Saxon Doncaster

After the Romans came the Saxons. It seemed that for a thousand years England was the battle ground of marauding invaders. No sooner had the last of the Romans taken his departure than the Saxons came. They were invited by the Britons, who, the moment they lost the protection of the Romans, found themselves the prey of their old enemies, the Picts and the Scots.

Now we are going to dismiss the Picts and the Scots from our picture. The Saxons drove them back, but, like many other conquerors, the Saxons were not satisfied with this. They laid claim to England. They conquered it. They established themselves in it. They took the Britons as slaves and serfs and those who escaped either went to the mountains of Wales and Cornwall or immigrated to France, and gave the name of Brittany to that part in which they settled.

Thus, we come to the end of the story of Picts, Scots and Britons. We are now concerned with the men who really made England. They were Germans, or Teutons as the Romans called them and they were known as Angles and

Saxons. Britain was a tempting land for invasion. On the East coast it lies right opposite Germany, and the River Humber invited the Saxon ships up its broad highway. From the Humber they ascended the River Don, which is tidal as far as Doncaster, and then we know that in the very early days of the Saxon invasion the lands on either side of the Don were soon in the hands of these hardy settlers from beyond the sea.

The Saxon invasion was more enduring than that of the Romans. When the Romans went, beyond their buildings, their laws and customs, little was left to influence the tide of history. The Saxons came to settle, and they never rested until the whole of the country was in their grasp. They grafted their language upon ours. They imposed their laws and customs upon the inhabitants who remained. They founded a new social system, and though the Norman invasion, 600 years later, was even a greater historical fact, it says something for the enduring character of the work of the Saxons that even the masterful Normans were unable to uproot it. It was the blending of the Saxon and the Norman that made the English race.

But before this came to pass, six long centuries had to roll on. Now, we are not going to write a history of Saxon England. If we were, we should describe at length how the Saxons divided the land into seven parts, known to historians as the period of Heptarchy, and how they established a King over each part. Doncaster was in the Northern kingdom, called Northumbria, and its first King was Edwin. There was a strong Saxon settlement around Doncaster, and it is believed that Edwin stayed in this town more than once. It is fairly certain that he was the first Saxon King to build a Christian church; and if the honour of having the first fell to York, it seems certain that the honour of having the second fell to Doncaster. Later, the seven Saxon Kingdoms were united as one and given the name England, and thus we see the origin of our race and the foundation of our state.

There are a thousand and one evidences of Saxon domination in the neighbourhood of Doncaster. Curiously enough, Doncaster was not their capital stronghold. They went four or five miles further up the Don and made Conisborough their fortress. They were established at Doncaster, and at Hexthorpe, which is now a busy manufacturing suburb of Doncaster, they founded a settlement, or Earldom known as the "soke", and from it their Earls ruled not only Doncaster, but Wheatley, Auckley, Austerfield, Rossington, Balby, Loversall and Warmsworth. At Conisborough and Tickhill they had residences, and Conisborough in particular, they made a Royal Centre. The name itself tells its story. It is derived from two old Saxon words "cyning" which means King and "burh" which translates fortified town. Later, the splendid romance of Conisborough will entitle it to a special chapter.

Meanwhile, though Hexthorpe was probably of little less importance than Doncaster, the Saxons may have had their church in what is now the town itself. It is believed that Doncaster's first church was built on what is now the centre of the town, very near the site of the present Corn Exchange. The Saxon Earl Goodwin was the first to be the Lord of the Soke of Hexthorpe, and thus he was the first great landlord of Doncaster – the first of a long line of illustrious names bound up very closely with the history of our town and also our country.

Saxon Doncaster need not detain us, although the period is full of interest. The Saxons were converted to Christianity in the time of Pope Gregory I, who sent Augustine with forty monks to spread the gospel. They had destroyed whatever remained of the Christianity introduced by the Romans, but when they themselves embraced the faith, they became zealous adherents, and Saxon churched started to spring up all over the land. In the North, as we have seen, the second of these Christian temples to rise was the one at Doncaster. For six centuries, Doncaster and its neighbourhood were occupied by the Saxons. Probably the town knew something of the terrors of the Danish invasion. It would know something of the great names of Saxon history of which that of King Alfred stands out as the most distinguished. It would benefit by the laws he made, the system of justice he introduced and the learning he brought to the people. For in those days, education was not the heritage of the poor. Even amongst the clergy there were many who could not read. It was Alfred the Great who altered this. He was, too, the founder of our Navy – the bulwark of our shores, the shield of our safety in years to come.

The church was placed upon a sure foundation by the Saxons. The Archbishoprics of York and London were founded. Parish churches began to dot the landscape. There was one at Doncaster, as we have seen, and there were others in the neighbourhood, although the actual Saxon remains, like those of the Romans are few and far between.

A picture of Saxon Doncaster would be deeply interesting. The standard of comfort was not very high. Even Kings slept upon straw and covered themselves with bearskins. The common people lived in hovels. Floors were covered with rushes, and the smoke from the fire had to escape as best it could by way of the door or through a hole in the roof. There was no lighting system, no water service, no sewerage arrangements – everything was crude, rough and uncomely. Yet it was a great period in English History as the race making a big step forward towards civilization. The Kingdom was divided into County's and Hundred's and the names still survive in our system of government. Sheriffs and Aldermen looked after the observance of the law, and the interests of the people were safeguarded by the institution of jury's and county courts. Indeed, even parliament was foreshadowed by the Saxons, for Alfred called a council in London twice per year, of nobles, bishops and landowners, to assist him in the government of the nation; and we may be sure that the Saxon Lords who held the lands around Doncaster, travelled to London in pomp and state, to lend their aid to the King in the good government of the country as a whole.

Chapter 4

Our Norman Ancestors

The coming of the Normans is the most important fact in English history. For a thousand years the history of our country is more or less obscure – we are always trying to look behind the veil and see what was happening. But when the Normans came, the veil was torn away forever. England stands revealed to all who wish to see it, and we can now follow every detail in the growth of our state, as well as in the growth of our town.

The Normans came to England in 1066. A thousand years after the Romans first came. Over 1000 years have passed since William I landed and won his great victory over the Saxons at Hastings, so that each of these periods covers more or less 1000 years. In these second thousand years, England was made; the British Empire was founded; and the half savage country the Romans left became the greatest civilized power the world, either ancient or modern, has ever seen. The Normans were Frenchmen from Normandy. They conquered the Saxons, who, as we have seen, were of German origin. In time, they blended together and became one people. Thus, an Englishman, if we go back to his origin, may be said to be part German and part French, with a mixture of British and Danish, and, perhaps a very slight infusion of Roman, for it is very likely that many Roman soldiers, magistrates, traders and other followers, married British women or founded families in the 350 years of the Roman occupation.

Thus, our language is very curious, yet wonderfully blended speech. If the reader wishes to see this for himself, let him take any twenty words out of a book then look at a dictionary. He will find that 5 or 6 of them, or even more, are Anglo-Saxon; some of them will be Norman, which means French, an odd 1 or 2 may be Danish; and the rest will be Latin (Roman) or Greek.

The Normans were a masterful people. They conquered England and they subjugated it – that is to say, they took complete possession of the land, the revenues, the taxes, the churches, and so on; they made new laws and institutions; they parcelled the country out among the great barons who had come with William and helped him win the day at Hastings. Thus we find many great families with distinctive Norman names, like the Fitzwilliam's of this district, boasting, and rightly too, that their ancestors "came over with the conqueror".
The Normans were very soon at Doncaster. The Saxons were turned out of their possessions and proud Normans were

installed. Sir Walter Scott's romance of Ivanhoe is one of the most stirring stories of the days of the Normans – when they lived in great castles, when they held jousts and tournaments, when they almost savagely oppressed the Saxons, and when monk and pilgrim, Knight and squire, robber and palmer were the picturesque figures of daily life. Well, Ivanhoe begins at Conisborough. Sir Walter Scott came to Sprotbrough, midway between Doncaster and Conisborough, to study the castle and the country around it; and he laid the opening scene of his immortal romance in the valley of the Don and in the great castellated pile which overlooks the river, and is the crowning glory of the Norman story as applied to Doncaster.

We have one admission to make – Doncaster town centre is poor in Norman remains. We have not a single Norman church or building in the town centre. Nearly everything has been swept away. But in every village around Doncaster relics abound. At Conisborough we have the castle. At Tickhill there is a castle still with the moat around it. At Roche Abbey we have the ruins of one of the most beautiful monastic buildings in Yorkshire. And finally, we have, within a few miles of Doncaster, some of the stateliest churches in the whole of the land. Tickhill church is noble enough for a minster; so is Hatfield; at Campsall, Burghwallis, Wadworth, Fishlake, Sprotbrough, Kirk Sandall, Barnburgh and a dozen other places, the Normans reared massive churches of solid masonry, with handsome square towers; and in these churches there are to be seen monuments, sculptures, carvings, screens all bearing the impress of the clever and reverent hands of the monkish builders. Fishlake has one of the most beautiful Norman porches in England; Sprotbrough has a 'Frith Stool' which is claimed to be one of the few existing seats in use in that far off period when criminals sought sanctuary in their parish churches.

So that even if Doncaster Centre is without its Norman church, even if we have no battlemented pile to frown over our streets and remind us of the imperious baron who held the people in serfdom for his master William, we strike a balance by claiming that the valley of the Don, and thence on to Selby, contains a host of churches which for beauty, dignity and massive simplicity will be hard to beat in any other part of the country.

One of the first acts of the Norman conquerors was to compile Doomsday (or Domesday) Book – a sort of survey of the whole country, showing the towns and villages, churches and halls, mills and weirs, fisheries and forests, and so forth, with their value, their revenue, their owners, and other details. This is the first book we turn to when we want actual information of the England that William conquered.

Doncaster is mentioned in Domesday Book – not as a town in itself, but as part of the 'soke' of Hexthorpe, or Easthorpe, meaning 'East Village'. It is curious that today, Doncaster is a bustling modern town with a Mayor and Council many hundred years old, while Hexthorpe is just a suburb drawn into the borough. Yet in Saxon days and early Norman days, it was Hexthorpe that was the centre and Doncaster that was near to it. There can be no doubt about this from the reading of the Domesday Book. There is a reference to the 'Manor of Hexthorpe' and then follows the remark that ' to this manor belongs the soccage (sokeage) of the men of Danecastre', implying, surely, that Doncaster was a mere part of the vast domain belonging to its Saxon owner. Still, there is no doubt that of the two, Doncaster was the more important place – with Saxon earthworks, a ditch or moat, certainly a church and mill, and probably even a castle.

After William I had conquered the land, he divided it up among his principal barons. He gave Doncaster and a great tract of the surrounding country to his half-brother, Robert, Earl of Moreton, and so we enter on a new era – when the Norman baron lived in the moated castle, when armed men rode with him when he fared forth, and when Saxon noble was despoiled of his rights and his possessions, and Saxon serf was the slave of his proud master.

We learn a great deal about Doncaster from the Domesday Book. Other adjoining towns and villages that still exist which find mention in that record are:

- Adwick-le-street
- Auckley
- Arksey
- Austerfield
- Badsworth
- Balby
- Barnburgh
- Barnby Dun
- Bentley
- Bilham
- Braithwell
- Bramwith
- Brodsworth
- Burghwallis
- Cadeby
- Campsall
- Cantley
- Clayton
- Clifton
- Conisborough
- Cusworth
- Dadesby (Tickhill)
- Denaby
- Edlington
- Elmsall
- Fishlake
- Frickley
- Goldthorpe

- Hampole
- Hexthorpe
- Hickleton
- Hooton Pagnell
- Kirkby
- Loversal
- Maltby
- Marr
- Melton-on-the-hill and West Melton
- Mexborough
- Norton
- Owston
- Pickburn
- Sandal
- Scawsby
- Skelbrooke
- Skellow
- Smeaton
- Sprotbrough
- Stainton
- Stainforth
- Sutton
- Thorne
- Thrybergh
- Thurnscoe
- Todwick
- Wadworth
- Warmsworth

- Wath
- Wheatley
- Wilsic

The Domesday Survey was made in the year 1086. The conqueror appointed commissioners, who went into every county to make inquiries concerning the land. They set down the name of the person who held the land in Edward's time, and how much it was then worth; by whom it was held at the time of the inquiry, and its worth; and also whether its value could be increased. Nothing was o be left out. The persons required to supply the information on their oaths were the Sheriffs, Lords of the Manors, Presbyters, Reeves, Bailiffs and others. The result of the inquisition was written in two books; these books are still preserved and known to the present generation by the name of Domesday Book. The thorough manner in which the conquerors great act was carried out by the commissioners is referred to by the Saxon chronicler as follows:

"So very narrowly he caused it to be traced out that there was not one single hide, nor one yard of land, nor even, it is shame to tell, though it seemed to him no shame to do, an ox, nor a cow, nor a swine was left, that was not set down in his writ. And all the writings were brought to him afterwards".

Copies of the survey have been published and Doncaster's entry is translated here:

"In Estorp (Hexthorpe), Earl Tosti had one manor of three carucates for geld and four ploughs may be there. Nigel has [it] of Count Robert. In the demesne, one plough and three villanes and three bordars with two ploughs. A church is there, and a priest having five bordars and one plough and two mills of thirty two shillings [annual value]. Four acres of meadow. Wood, pasturable, one leuga and a half in length and one leuga in breadth. The whole manor, two leugae and a half in length and one leuga and a half in breadth. T.R.E., it was woth eighteen pounds, now twelve pounds. To this manor belongs this soke – Donecastre (Doncaster) two carucates, in Wermesford (Warmsworth) on carucate, in Ballebi (Balby) two carucates, in Geureshale (Loversall) two carucates, Oustrefeld (Austerfield) two carucates and Alcheslei (Auckley) two carucates. Together fifteen carucates for geld, where eighteen ploughs may be. Now [there is] in the demesne one plough and twenty four villanes and thirty seven bordars and forty sokemen. These have twenty seven ploughs, wood, pasturable in places, in places unprofitable"

Doncaster is mentioned six times in the survey, but in no instance is it distinguished as a manor. It may be conjectured that it was included in the manor of Hexthorpe; it does not seem probable that ever there was either a church or a water mill at Hexthorpe, therefore it is not an unreasonable assumption that the church and the two mills entered as belonging to Hexthorpe were really situated in the adjoining town, or vill, of Doncaster. One reason why Doncaster was comprehended in Hexthorpe has been offered, and as it has about it the element of probability it is included here. Namely, that the Manor House (aula) where dwelt the Lords steward, or seneschal, was situated in Hexthorpe, and that the greater part of Doncaster was an integral part of the Hexthorpe manor. It was no uncommon thing for a village to belong in parts to several manors; a part of Doncaster was of the manor of Wheatley, and another part was of the manor of Edlington. The latter part was held by Malagar under William de Perci, one of the great Norman Barons. It is a remarkable fact that Wheatley, in the parish of Doncaster, and just referred to as including in its manorial territory part of ancient Doncaster, contained two small manors.

At this distance of time and the lack of authoritative records, it is impossible to say what the exact social status of the Domesday inhabitants of Doncaster were. It cannot now be determined whether there ever dwelt within its precincts a free village community, as evolved out of the ancient mark, or what was the precise nature of the influences from Roman times onwards which shaped the character and destiny of its people. Doubtless, a remnant of Roman law and customs survived. The influence of Saxon and Danish settlers would modify old usages and create new conditions. The Norman took hold of things as he found them, and moulded them as far as prudent on the lines of the feudal system for the special benefit of the new monarchy and its attendant train of adventurous supporters.

By the aid of the Domesday census we are enabled to get an interesting fact, namely, that the Hexthorpe soke contained a proportionately large number of a superior class of tenants, as compared with the tenants of the estates in the West Riding of Yorkshire. In the West Riding there were 268 sokemen, 1763 villanes and 1097 bordars. In Hexthorpe the numbers were 40 sokemen, 24 villanes and 27 bordars. Opinions differ as to the general conditions under which these sokemen (sochmanni) held their holdings, and what was their exact social status. All agree that they were a superior class to that of the villanes (villani), but whether their position was only a little above that of the villanes, or whether they ranked equal with that of the burgesses of Domesday Book are question we cannot answer here. The name is mostly confined to districts formerly under Danish influence; for this reason it has been suggested that they were of Danish origin. Probably by far the greater number of the Hexthorpe sokemen lived at Doncaster. It was to the descendants of these men that King Richard granted a charter confirming to them "all the liberties and free customs" enjoyed by them and their ancestors for a length of time now lost in obscurity. The Doncaster part of the soke gradually evolved into a borough, and a borough that continues to evolve today, we may even see Doncaster evolve into a city in the not too distant future, time will tell.

The pre-Domesday holder of the Lordship, Earl Tosti, was the son of Godwin, Earl of the West Saxons. He was deposed and banished and went over to Flanders. A short time after this he joined the King of Norway in an expedition against England. The combined fleets entered the Humber and proceeded up the Ouse near to York. Tosti was killed at the battle of Stamford Bridge on the 25th September, 1066, and was buried at York.

Robert, Count of Mortain in Normandy and Earl of Cornwall in England was, on the mother's side, half brother to the conqueror. He was at the battle of Hastings and was handsomely rewarded for his service there. The number of manors given to him is variously stated, but it must have approached near to 800. No injustice will be done to his memory if we say that he was a troublesome fellow and evidently well versed in the art of mischief making. His brother Odo, bishop of Bayeux and Earl of Kent, had been banished in the conquerors time, but had been allowed to return when William Rufus became King. Robert joined Odo in an attempt to depose the King, for which he was banished and his estates forfeited.

Nigel Fossard was one of the principal under-tenants of Count Robert, of whom he held some 91 manors. Hexthorpe was his chief holding in Yorkshire. It appears highly probable that on the forfeiture of Count Robert's estates, Nigel was advanced to the dignity of a tenant in capite, that is, to hold his lands directly from the King, and not through a second person as he had previously done. He appears to have been what would now be termed a generous man. Included in his gifts to the Abbot and Convent of St Mary, York, was the gift of the church of Doncaster and neighbourhood. He was succeeded by his son Adam, who founded the priory of Hode (Hood Grange, Yorkshire).

Robert, who succeeded him paid a fine of 500 marks to the King to repossess the Lordship of Doncaster, "which he had parted to the King to hold in demesne for twenty years". The reason for the surrender to the King and the high price for the repossession is not apparent. It has been suggested that Robert had not paid the whole of the fee due to the King on his succeeding to the patrimonial inheritance, hence the lease and release; but it was not unlikely that it was a transaction to enable the King to raise some needed cash. William, his son and heir, succeeded him. He was the last of the Fossards in the male line. He was one of the northern barons who fought against the scots in the battle of the standard. In 1142 he was with Stephen's forces against the Empress Maude at the battle of Lincoln and was taken prisoner. On the collection of scuttage, a tax paid in lieu of Military service etc, by those who held land by Knights service, he paid £12; a fairly large sum in those days, at other times he paid £21 and a further sum of £31 10s, the last amount was levied upon him because he was not in the Irish Wars. He was especially exempted from contributing for the redemption of King Richard I. He left a daughter, Joan, who was married to Robert de Turnham.

A Robert de Turnham had two sons, Robert and Stephen. It was Robert the younger who married Joan Fossard. He was a crusader, and was reputed to be a powerful and valiant man. Some historians say that he died on an expedition to the Holy Land but there is no evidence for this statement. He appears to be with the King in the Holy Land, and was entrusted to bring the King's harness back to England. For the services on that journey he was discharged from the payment of scuttage levied for the Kings ransom. Being in the Kings confidence he probably exerted himself in obtaining from the king, a charter confirming to the burgesses of Doncaster whatever ancient privileges they then possessed. He obtained a grant of two more days to be added to the fair that had anciently been kept at his manor of Doncaster in County Ebor, upon the eve and day of St James the apostle. At his death in 1199, the yearly value of the lands held by him in right of Joan, his wife, was entered at £411.

9s. 2d. He left a daughter, Isabell, who became a ward of the King.

There was a long line of Peter de Mauley's who successively held the Lordship of Doncaster. The first of these is said to have committed an infamous crime at the instigation of King John. On the death of King Richard, his brother John, "knowing that he could not succeed him by reason that Arthur, son of Geoffry of Brittany, was alive, got Arthur into his power and implored Peter de Mauley, his esquire, to murder him and in reward gave him the heir of the barony of Mulgref". Some doubts have arisen as to the truthfulness of this statement. If Mauley really did commit the act at the instigation of John, and was led to expect that he would receive the Kings ward to wife and the free enjoyment of her lands, he was deceived; for Peter de Mauley paid a fine of 7000 marks "for entrance to the inheritance of the daughter of Robert de Turnham". He gave the body of his wife to be buried at the Abbey of Meux, Holderness, endowing the Abbey with a rent of Sixty shillings per year. He died before 1241. In 1247 the King took the homage of his heir, Peter, for all his father's lands. Some six years later this Peter de Mauley obtained a charter of Free Warren in his demesne lands, which included Doncaster. He died in 1279. The next Peter paid £100 relief for all lands held of the King in capite of the inheritance of William Fossard. From a document from 1279 we catch a glimpse of a part of the Mauley holdings for which the above relief was paid:

Donecastre..........rent of assizes by the year, £17. There is at Donecastre four mills, and at Hexthorpe one mill, which are worth by the year, forty marcs. Market-tole (tollon fori) of Donecastre is worth twenty marcs; also the court of Donecastre, 60 shillings, sum, £60. Of which the Lord, Peter de Mauley six years ago gave to Peter, his son and heir (ad ipsam dotand) £7. 10s. 9d. yearly; and so there remained in his hands at the time of his death £52. 9s. 3d.

The same Peter, styled the fourth, obtained license of the King to alienate to the Earl of Surrey ".......the manor and town of Donecastre, with the appurtenances, and the advowson of the church of Rosyngton, which are held of us in capite, or in chief, as is said..........." The charter is dated March 24th, 1332. The grant was for the Earls life, with reversion to Peter de Mauley the fifth or his heirs. Peter the fifth was 21 at his father's death. During his father's lifetime he received a Knighthood with Prince Edward and many others. It was this Mauley who released the town from certain customary payments, an extremely important act. He was 29 when he died in Doncaster. The eighth and last Peter died without issue. He left two sisters, one became the wife of Sir J Bigot, knight, but there was no issue of the marriage. The other married George Salvin Esq. The Salvins do not appear to have been in a hurry to assert a claim to any rights held by the Mauley's in Doncaster. The manorial and other rights appear to have reverted quietly to the corporation. Subsequently, a descendant of the Salvins put the corporation to considerable trouble and anxiety.

Conisbrough Castle was built by Hamelin Plantagenet, half brother of Henry II in the 1170's. The magnificent keep and parts of the gatehouse and curtain wall remain. By late Tudor times it was owned by George Carey, 1st Lord Hunsdon, high steward of the Borough of Doncaster, cousin to Queen Elizabeth and Lord Chamberlain. Its nearest neighbour was Tickhill castle over the limestone ridge to the south west.

Post 1066 the Normans harried the north, dispensed Saxon manors and estates to Williams supporters and built a rapid series of Motte and Bailey castles (with wooden keeps on a central mound and a wooden palisade to defend the inner bailey around the keep). One such was at Doncaster near the later St George's church, others at Conisbrough and Tickhill. Some of these were soon replaced by stone keeps and curtain walls, but not at Doncaster. Conisbrough had a much more dominant hill top site overlooking a Don ford and hence became a major defensive stronghold with the building of a huge 90ft high cylindrical keep of magnesian limestone in the 1170's. It was similar to the castle at Mortemer, near Dieppe in France, also a Warenne stronghold. It was soon to have a curtain wall bailey with defensive tower and a barbican (gatehouse), much of which still survives.

It is South Yorkshire's most impressive military monument, as unlike Pontefract Castle and Tickhill, it survived demolition by the parliamentarians during the Civil War of the 1640's, plundering of stone was also inhibited by 18th and 19th century antiquarians. Now under the management of English Heritage, it has car parking facilities, a visitors centre, and opportunity to walk the dry moat ditch, explore the walls and climb the keep. The keep is one of the largest in the country and affords stunning views over the entire Don valley. Little wonder that Sir Walter Scott took inspiration for his book Ivanhoe after spending time in the immediate area.

At the time of the Norman invasion, Conisbrough with its Saxon stone church was the centre of a huge manorial Lordship and parish belonging to King Harold. At the time of the Domesday Book's writing, the 'honour' extended south to the Nottinghamshire border with manors to the east at Hatfield, Thorne and Fishlake supplying the estate with over 1000 eels per year from the wetlands in mediaeval times.

William I (the Conqueror) gave the Conisbrough honour to William de Warenne from near Dieppe who had been one of his close confidants at the Battle of Hastings. It was

Warenne's descendant Hamelin Plantagenet who built the new stone castle in the 1170's. The Warenne's were also granted the Sandal honour near Wakefield, where they erected another stone fortress.

Conisbrough township prospered in the lee of the castle and its St Peter's church was given a Norman make-over and contains one of the earliest St George sculptural reliefs. The castle developed its own deer park. 'Conisbrough' means 'Kings Fort' and the name may date back to a Northumbrian Saxon Earl's defensive structure on the border with Mercia. As a Norman fortress it formed part of a strategic network – Lincoln, Newark, Sheffield, Pontefract, Sandal, Tickhill, York, and Spofford (near Harrogate). When John de Warenne, 8th Earl of Surrey died without heirs in 1347 the Conisbrough estates reverted to the Crown. Edward III gave it to the Duke of York in 1461. Richard, the then Duke of York's son became Edward IV and Conisbrough again became a Royal Castle.

The Crown had held the castle between 1322 and 1326 when Edward II had Earl Thomas Warenne executed at Pontefract castle for leading a northern rebellion. Edward II stopped briefly at Conisbrough in November 1322, but whether accompanied by his gay young lover, Piers Galveston is not recorded!

During the Tudor period the castle was neglected and degenerated into a crumbling ruin, it was not good enough to be defended in the 1640's Civil War, perhaps this is the reason that it has survived to this day. It remained for a long period in the hands of the Carey family after a grant of ownership by Henry VIII.

While we are writing of Conisborough Castle, the mind naturally leaps to that other castle at Tickhill – not so imposing a monument, but equal in historic interest.

When Normans came to the valley of the Don they swarmed over the countryside. The district around Doncaster was soon a populous Norman settlement. Tickhill is only seven miles away, and a castle was soon raised there, for the lands were given by William the Conqueror to one of his barons named Roger de Busli. And so Tickhill, now a very small market town with a long, straggling main street, comes into our picture as a Norman stronghold.

Nobody today would think that Tickhill had a crowded history. A visitor might pass through it and never even see its castle. Unlike Conisborough, which stands upon a bold and commanding hill seen from every approach, the site of Tickhill Castle is comparatively low and, as it is surrounded by walls and is now in the private grounds of a family residence, it may quite easily be overlooked.

This would be a pity. For not only is the castle of deep interest, but it has something that even Conisborough lacks – it is surrounded, or at least partly surrounded, by a moat or ditch which still contains water. The fact that this moat may be seen by a visitor standing in the street and looking over the boundary wall adds to the novelty of the situation. The idea of a motorist pulling up in little Tickhill and looking over a wall and beholding a moat which, in an instant, carries the mind back to the feudal days of long ago, touches the imagination – linking up the ancient and the modern.

Tickhill Castle was built by Roger de Busli in the first few years of the Norman occupation. It was altered and improved in later years. Henry I added the gatehouse, and Henry II built the keep. The gatehouse still exists, though the mound on which the keep was reared is now without what must have been an imposing structure. There are no remains which are at all to be compared with the castle at Conisborough.

Its history, however, is important. In the reign of Henry I (1100-1135), its owner rebelled and lost his possessions, and Tickhill became the property of the Crown. King Henry II and his Queen Eleanor stayed there, and Eleanor founded a chapel within it, giving it the name of St. Nicholas.

On three occasions the castle was besieged. King John grasped it while Richard I was a prisoner on the continent, and when Richard returned he sent a force to re-take it. In Ivanhoe there is a graphic story of how Richard stormed Torquilstone Castle, and it is not at all unlikely that it was Tickhill Castle which Scott had in his mind at the time.

It was in the reign of Edward II that the castle stood its second siege. The Earl of Lancaster attacked it, but failed to take it; and after he had been defeated at Boroughbridge, he was executed at Pontefract. So that what with Tickhill, Boroughbridge and Pontefract, Thomas, Earl of Lancaster, did very badly in Yorkshire. Curiously enough, as though by a turn of the wheel of fortune, the castle that had been so disastrous to one Lancaster came into the possession of another. John O'Gaunt, "time-honour'd Lancaster", as Shakespeare calls him, assumed the ownership of Tickhill at the time of Edward III, and it thus became part of the vast estates of the Duchy of Lancaster.

The last siege of all was during the Civil War. Tickhill, naturally, was on the side of the King. When the Roundheads were sweeping all before them in the North, they rode into Tickhill, and the garrison speedily surrendered the castle. The Earl of Manchester was in command of the Roundheads, or Parliamentarians, and he had stayed in Doncaster before setting out for Tickhill. It is always said that Oliver Cromwell himself was with this section of the Parliamentary army; and if it be so, then the great Oliver had an association with both Doncaster and Tickhill.

The castle was, in the time this piece was written (c. 1920) under the ownership of the Earl of Scarbrough, and his Lordship was as careful to see that no harm befell its relics as he was of the more beautiful Roche Abbey, only a few miles further on.

There is another memorial at Tickhill which links this little town with the past. In the high street there are the remains of a quaint pillared and porticoed building of timber and plaster, which was built as far back as 1470. It is known as St. Leonard's Hospital. It was founded even earlier than the date given, for there is a document of the time of Henry III (1236), which proves that it was then a hospital for lepers. If any part of the original building does remain, that it should have survived all these centuries, and the more massive castle have disappeared with the exception of its gatehouse, is one of the curious facts of history.

Tickhill people are very proud of their little town. There castle links them with Norman baron and Crusader king; their hospital of St. Leonard carries the mind back to the days when the monks were not only an order of religious men, but were the healers of the sick; and its church, one of the most magnificent in South Yorkshire, has a noble tower which, if the reading of its armorial sculpture be correct, was built between 1373 and 1399 by no less a personage than that same John O'Gaunt, Duke of Lancaster, who was the Lord of the castle and its manor.

Today there are no signs of the bustle and animation that must have prevailed in those early times. Tickhill is quiet, calm and reserved. It stands in the midst of a beautiful park-like country, with Roche Abbey not far away on one side and the graceful Abbey Church of Blythe on the other. The collieries are being opened out; and a mile or two away is Harworth where a German syndicate was sinking a coal-pit when the Great War broke out in 1914. The men were promptly interned, and the sinking of the pit was stopped; and, later, the site and the workings were acquired by the owners of the Bentley Pit at Doncaster.

So, just as Tickhill streets will never again witness the colour and pomp of mediaeval life, so will they never again resound with the foreign talk of German pit-sinkers sent here on behalf of a company who coolly intended to take our coal from beneath our feet.

There were other castles in the area too, castle's that the onslaught of nature and time have not been so kind to. We must remember that not all of these structures were constructed of stone. I think of the fortified manor houses of Scawthorpe.

When William the Conqueror came to England in 1066, one of his important supporters, a certain Nigel Fossard was rewarded for his service to the king in his battle against Harold. Part of his award was lands in this area; one of those manors was that of Arksey. Scawthorpe and Bentley came under the umbrella of Arksey and Fossard placed his stamp on the area by building fortified manor houses. One of these houses was Radcliffe Moat, a motte and bailey castle between Scawthorpe and Bentley (now intersected by the Leeds railway line), the other, and Radcliffe's predecessor, was the scheduled ancient monument at Castle Hills.

The monument comprised a 4-5m high motte with a kidney-shaped inner bailey to the north and a sub-rectangular outer bailey to the east. The inner bailey was approximately 30m across and the outer bailey approximately 70m x 40m. On the west side, between the motte and inner bailey, a 2m high oval mound formed the end of the rampart circling the motte to the south west and has since been interpreted as a defended approach to the monument.

The complexity of the earthworks suggests that it was a monument of some importance. Certainly it commanded the manor of Langthwaite (later Hangthwaite), one of six held by

Nigel Fossard in 1086 from the Count of Mortain. The de Langthwaites seem to have become an important family, whose name appears in many northern documents. It was in the later medieval period that the manor was moved approximately 300m east to Radcliffe.

The immediate area was essentially a medium sized village and recent finds in the soil adjoining the castle mounds strongly suggest this to be case.

All these defensive buildings suggest the borough was a place of some importance. Natural resources and minerals made the industry quite rich. Up to this point most of the profits had been creamed off by the Crown. But, what if we could pay a rent to the Crown for the town and then employ our own folk to run it for us? Enter our first Royal Charter.

It is an interesting occupation to delve into the history of our old town. There is so much fiction, overlaid with so much legend, that it is difficult to discover the exact amount of truth at the bottom layer. Fortunately, in the case of Doncaster, we have invaluable records, and we shall find in these that we are able to piece together the story of Doncaster's growth into a municipal borough in complete and convincing fashion.

Doncaster today is a municipal borough. That is to say, it is governed by a mayor and corporation. They sit together, and may be described as our local parliament. They look after our health and sanitation; they provide us with water, gas, electricity, and tramway cars; they make by-laws for the good government of the town, and when the by-laws have been sanctioned by parliament in London, they have all the force and authority as Acts of Parliament themselves. Moreover, the local town council has power to levy rates to pay for the upkeep of the town's institutions, to pay the wages of municipal officials, policemen and other public servants; and once these rates are laid by the town council, or levied as the phrase puts it, and are confirmed by the magistrates, burgesses are compelled to pay them, and may be summoned to the police court if they refuse.

These, then, are the powers of a town council. Where do they get these powers from? Who gave the people of Doncaster the right and liberty to elect a mayor and councillors? In other words, when did Doncaster become a self-governing borough?

The answer is interesting. Doncaster is one of the very oldest boroughs in the whole of England. We have seen that it was a town in Saxon days, and that the Normans continued it as such. In the reigns of the early Norman kings, the two Williams, Stephen, and the two Henrys, the Doncaster burgesses held their town from the king for the annual fee of £60. That is a rough-and-ready way of describing the fact that one Adam Fitz Swein is known to have paid the king a sum of £60 a year on account of Doncaster; and one receipt shows us that on one occasion, at any rate, he and others paid this rental in quarterly sums of £15. This Adam Fitz Swein was one of the lords of the honours of Pontefract and Tickhill, and it is easy to imagine that Doncaster had, by lease or other means, come into his scheme of ownership.

The importance of this fact is that it definitely places Doncaster in the list of Norman towns. It was no village, no cluster of cottages, to be valued at £60 a year in the money of those days. If the Fitz Swein family paid this rental to the throne, we may be sure that they got it back again out of the pockets of the burgesses. Thus Doncaster was no mean place when the Plantagenet kings sat upon England's throne.

But what fixes Doncaster position even more definitely than this rental to the king, is the first charter granted to the burgesses by Richard I, or Cœur de Lion, as every scholar likes to call him, who took the throne in 1189. In the fifth year of his reign he granted Doncaster its first charter which gave us the royal permission to be called a town. We put the date at 1194 and now Doncaster has been a borough for over 800 years.

This places us amongst the oldest boroughs in the United Kingdom. Our mayors are proud of that fact. Every year great municipal banquets are held in London and the big cities of England, such as Leeds, Sheffield, Manchester and so forth. Very often the mayors of Doncaster are invited, and when they come back they relay with pride how they were treated – not because of themselves, but because they represented a borough which stretches right back through the centuries to the great days of the brilliant crusading king, Richard I, Cœur de Lion, Richard the Lionheart.

Now, this charter is not a very long one but is so very important. It surely and firmly establishes our position.

"Richard, by the grace of God, King of England, Duke of Normandy and Aquitain, Earl of Anjou, to the Archbishops, Bishops, Abbots, Earls, Barons, Justices, Sheriffs, Stewards, Governors, and Headboroughs; and all his ministers, and faithful subjects, GREETING".
"Know Ye, that we have granted, and by our present Charter have confirmed to our burgesses of Danecastre, their Sco, Soke, or Soak of Danecastre, to have and to hold of us and our heirs by the ancient rent, which at the time was rendered to us, and over and besides, twenty five marks of silver, to be paid us annually, with the ancient rent, that they may answer the marks to us at our Exchequer. And, for this our grant, they have given us fifty

marks of silver. Wherefore, we will and firmly command,
that the said, our burgesses of Danecastre, may have and
hold their aforesaid soke, with the town of Danecastre, in
manner aforesaid, effectually, and peaceably; freely and
quietly; fully and honourably, with all the Liberties and
Free Customs to the same appertaining; so that none
hereupon may them disturb. These persons being witnesses.
– H. Archbishop of Canterbury, R. Archdeacon of Hereford,
William de Warren, Osbert the son of Hervey, Simon de
Pateshelle, Ric Barre, Simon de Kimbe, and very many
others. Given by the land of Master Eustecius, Dean of
Salisbury, then officiating in the place of Chancellor, the
twenty second day of May, at Toke, or Tuke, in the fifth year
of our reign."

This document is a landmark in Doncaster's history as a
borough. The burgesses paid fifty marks of silver for it. We
have seen that Adam Fitz Swein paid £60 a year rental to the
king for Doncaster. In future, the burgesses were to pay that
sum directly to the throne, with the addition of another five
marks of silver. For this they held the liberties and free
customs of the town; and in order that none should question
their right, this charter contains the Royal command, "So
that none hereupon may them disturb".

Thus Doncaster, as we say, has been a town by Royal Charter
for at least 726 years. As charters go, it is not a very long one,
and it does not contain the grant of many privileges. There is

no record of a Mayor, or 'Headborough', or any other public official; and it says nothing about markets, or common rights, or any other privileges held by the burgesses. But it must be distinctly noticed that its effect is to confirm anything of the sort already held by the town. That is to say, Doncaster was a town before this charter was granted. It was rented from the town at £60 a year. In return for that sum it undoubtedly possessed many of the privileges of a town. All that Richard's charter does is this – it makes the payment of the rental direct from the burgesses to the king; and that the rental had been long paid is proved by the fact that the charter speaks of it as an 'ancient rent'.

We are justified, therefore, in assuming:

1. that Doncaster was an old and honoured town when Richard came to the throne in 1189
2. that it was already paying rent which had so long continued as to be spoken of as 'ancient'
3. that it enjoyed 'liberties and free customs' which were confirmed and ratified by this charter

In other words, Doncaster was not made a town even by Richard I, he recognised it as a town and confirmed it in lawful possession of its liberties, its privileges and its customs.

Nowadays, when a town receives a charter from the monarch, or its ancient rights are amended or enlarged, it makes for great rejoicing. In 1914 Doncaster's old borough was enlarged to take in a great deal of suburban territory. These things are usually the occasion of a great scheme of public rejoicing – banquets, processions, fireworks, speeches, and so forth. How interesting it would be if we could look through the ages that hide the past and see what the burgesses of Doncaster did when Richard's charter was received in the town! Did special envoys bring it to the town? Was it met at the gate by the headmen of the borough? Did they pace the streets in solemn state? Did the bells ring out as the precious parchment was carried to the town-house and curiously inspected by the city father, as they handled its seal and tried to read its crabbed writing?

We shall never know. But one thing we do know – that Richard I by his charter, confirmed Doncaster's position amongst the eldest boroughs of our land, and for that reason Doncaster people should always hold his memory in high regard.

It will be news to many Doncaster readers that this charter is still in existence. It is a sheet of parchment about 8 inches wide and 10 inches long. It is written in Normandy-French, in a clear clerkly hand; and though the penmanship is 726 years old, every word is still distinct. It is kept in the strong-room of the town clerk's office, along with all the other charters in the possession of the local authorities.

We are entitled to ask: How many towns in England are able to produce an original charter older than this, or even as old?

Chapter 5

Doncaster Takes Shape

It was in the reigns of the early Norman Kings that the towns of England began to take their rise. The country was so unsettled, Norman robbers and Saxon outlaws made life so hard for the people at large, that the shelter of towns was sort as a refuge from the lawlessness of the countryside. There was this to be said in favour of the towns – that each had its lord, and though he himself ruled the townspeople with a rod of iron, he could at any rate be depended upon to afford them protection from others.

In those days, Doncaster began to take shape. If we could pierce the veil, we should see the serfs bringing corn and cattle into the town; we should see the townsmen pursuing their trades in peace, and forming themselves into those guilds which, in later generations, were such a powerful factor in the trades and industries of the land; we should see the parish church as the centre for religious life; just as the castle was the centre of social life; we should see the town defended by gates at all the principal approaches; we should see hospitals and friaries and almshouses springing up at various points; we should see the honest burgesses gradually forming themselves into what later became the borough and the municipality, with mayor and aldermen, and town clerk and beadle; we should, in fact, see the gradual growth of the Doncaster we know today.

But before that came about the town went through many changes. We wonder if there is a town in England which has been so often totally destroyed as Doncaster has? In 1204 a great fire consumed everything that was not made of stone. Only one relic, apart from public churches and buildings, seems to have been left standing, and that was the cross in Hallgate, a newer version of which still stands on or very near to the site.

England, and particularly its highways, used to be dotted with crosses, and it was quite in keeping with the spirit of the age that a cross should be erected on the Great North Road, at the top of the hill, at the entrance to the town. The old cross stood for many centuries. The one now in its place is but a copy and was put up in 1793. It is named Hall Cross and is one of the most familiar objects both to townspeople and to travellers through the town; and there is a touch of sentiment in the thought that it perpetuates the predecessor which may have stood on or near that site for over 600 years. The original cross was erected by Ote de Tilli, who was steward to the Earl of Conisborough and who lived in the 12th century. After standing there all those hundreds of years, a link with the days of the Normans, it was taken down by the Corporation as part of a street improvement scheme in 1793, and the Hall Cross we know today was erected in its place.

Doncaster always had its castle. The Romans had one, and certainly the Saxons had one, and it is very probable that the Normans built one too. Nothing is more amazing than the fact that not a single stone marks the site of any one of them. In many towns the castle is still the show place. Its crumbling towers and battlemented walls are the epitome of local history. But though Doncaster must of had 2 or 3 castles, probably upon the same site, nothing remains to attest to their shape or grace. That they stood near the present parish church of St George is about all we know. When Leland came to write his account of the town, in the 16th century, he said that the church "stands in the very area where on the castle of the town stood, long since decayed". He could trace the dykes or ditches, and the foundations of the wall; but the castle itself had gone, swept clear away; and save for occasional references in title deeds of neighbouring lands, there would be little to show that we even had a castle at all.

There were mills upon the river Don, and the church of St Mary Magdalene stood in what is now the Market Place. We believe that it was older than the parish church, and perhaps it actually was the parish church before St George's was built. The entrances to the town had some sort of gates, though the frequency of the word "gate" in street naming is not to be taken in its literal sense. We have today St Sepulchre Gate, Fishergate, Hallgate, Marshgate, Frenchgate, Baxter gate, St George's gate, east and west Laith gates, and even other; but it is not likely that all these thoroughfares were guarded by actual gates of timber and iron. The word "gate" was often used to mean "road", or "approach", and it is probably in that sense that we should often regard it.

Still, the main approaches to the town undoubtedly had gates, and the one by the river bridge was the scene of many a fierce fight. King John issued a warrant to have the town enclosed according to the course of the ditch, and to have the bridge fortified, and we know that this was done and that the tower by the bridge was taken and re-taken many times in the course of the desperate fights which were such a common feature of the life of the middle ages.

The old Mill Bridge over the Don has a history of its own. History is often made in the region of bridges. It is here that city fathers have declaimed against civil oppressors; it is here that religious reformers have thundered against what they call abuses; it is here that armed bands have made assault upon tower and gate and been repulsed, or not, as the case may be, by the defenders. Yes; a towns bridge is often the repository of a great deal of local history, and it is only to repeat the lament we make about most other antiquities when we add that the early bridges crossing the Don at the approach to the town have been swept out of existence until nothing remains but vivid fancy to enable us to reconstruct the picture.

The Don and the Cheswold run almost side by side on the northern border of the town, and each has its bridge. There was a House of Greyfriars nearby, and one of the bridges was guarded by a tower or gatehouse. Then there was a chapel, called the chapel of St Mary, just as several other towns had their bridge chapels. In other words, the bridge was a fortified gateway.

There are many references to the more important of these two bridges, St Mary's. When King John issued his warrant ordering the town of Doncaster to be enclosed with palings, he also directed that the bridge should have a barbican erected upon it, "to defend the town, if need be". Here we see the importance of the bridge in the scheme of the towns defence. Nowadays, as traffic rumbles across it, and the electric tram-cars thunder above the gurgling water and drown the booming of the weir, we find it hard to realise that this peaceful spot was once the scene of many a fierce engagement; that the heads of many brave men have been impaled above the gate as warnings to the venturesome; that tower and barbican looked out across the road and bade defiance to the enemy; and that when the gate was slammed and bolted, and archers mounted guard within the tower, it was opened only for urgent travellers or at the orders of a superior force.

Then there were the friaries, or religious houses of the monks. The Carmelites had one in the centre of town and the Franciscans, or Greyfriars, had another. Greyfriars road still perpetuates the name of one of these religious houses. It is now devoted to tramway sheds, electricity works, and public swimming baths; but the very name is a reminder that these old monkish orders had their establishments in our town. No sandaled friar walks our streets today. He has gone the way of the baron and the crusader, the serf and the villain, the palmer and the wandering minstrel; but so long as Greyfriars road endures we shall always have the name to connect us with those picturesque figures of the past.

Then there was the town ditch, or moat. It crossed St Sepulchre gate, Printing Office Street, Cleveland Street, Silver Street, to Sunny Bar – from the river back to the river; and if you follow the route in your mind's eye, you will gather that ancient Doncaster, or at least all of it that was included within this area, was of very limited extent compared with the present widely-flung borough boundaries.

Thus we are able to obtain a fairly accurate idea of what the town was like in mediaeval times. It was not a walled town, but it was surrounded by a moat, and this, in turn, was strengthened by the "palings", erected by order of King John. There were, in all probability, four actual "gates" to hold up undesirable travellers, and the principal of these was that fortified tower on St Mary's bridge over the Don. Two churches, a castle in ruins, hospitals and monastic houses, completed what may be called the public buildings. Then there were the timbered and wattled houses of the people – not a very magnificent picture, but true to the spirit of the genius of the age.

Outside Doncaster the country was mostly forest and marsh. Wherever there was a clearing, there was a village; and we may be sure that the Normans did not leave any village long without a church. To the south of the town, Sherwood Forest came almost to the edge of the old borough, and Robin Hood must often have come through Doncaster. His principal exploits were carried out in the glades of far-stretching Sherwood; but north of the town there was much wild heath, and also forest, in the region known as Barnesdale, and Robin Hood is credited with more than one merry jest in that neighbourhood. Moreover, he died at Kirklees, near Brighouse, and to get there from Sherwood he would almost surely have had to pass through Doncaster.

Many great names are associated with Doncaster, but it is safe to say that there is no name around which fiction and legend have gathered such a cluster of romance of that which adorns the name of Robin Hood.

Chapter 6

Early Religion

All Saints - Arksey

According to the Doomsday Book of 1086 the lands surrounding what was then the very tiny settlement of Arksey and Bentley were held by Roger de Busli, an officer in the invading Norman army of William the Conqueror. The land was low lying and so was a very marshy corner of Doncaster. In about 1120 the highest area in Arksey was chosen to be the site of a church (although there was probably an earlier Saxon church on the same site) of substantial size and importance, to demonstrate Roger de Busli's ownership of the land and his family prestige. The church was built of stone and in the shape of a cross by Norman masons, men who had brought with them the distinctive architectural style that in Europe is called 'Romanesque'. At the centre of the cross shaped building, de Busli had built, a single storey tower. This tower has only small, narrow, round-headed windows. Something like 80% of this original church survives within the building we see today.

Adam de Newmarche, Lord of Arksey, (the grandson of Roger de Busli) began extending the building in 1180. The extensions consisted of a second storey to the tower, with aisles both north and south of the Nave. This work took until 1220 to complete. The north aisle was added first, with most of the nave wall being replaced by three round columns, each column having octagonal capitals and double chamfered arches between. A large round-headed archway was built in the west wall of the north transept for access to the north aisle. The remains of a Norman window are still visible in this wall, it is narrow, little more than a slit, and has a round-headed arch of Norman architecture. The south aisle was not as large an extension as the north aisle at this time, and was built as a narrow aisle, possible to create a chantry chapel. The pillars of the south aisle are octagonal in section and differ greatly from those of the north aisle. When one looks at the top of the wall of the staircase of the tower, at the east end of the south aisle, deep grooves can be seen into which had been inserted the roof of the narrow aisle. After the second storey addition the weight of the tower was now doubled and so a fine set of four arches were constructed in order to transmit the weight of this addition through to the load bearing foundations, the arches, built in the style of 'Early English' are perhaps the finest architectural feature of the entire church.

The north east chapel, now housing the church organ, was built around 1300 as indicated by the style of its east window. The south east chapel, which somewhat oddly projects a few feet east of the chancel, was built later in about 1400. Its present windows were constructed at that time. The chancel's north and south walls were opened out in the same century, with the fine arches we see today. Fragments of the original window openings may still be seen.

During the middle of the 15th century, the south aisle was widened to be as we see it today, and the porch was built. This completed the extensions to the church at ground level, but a spire was added onto the tower at a later date.

Inside the church there are many fine Jacobean furnishings. The font cover is dated 1662 and incorporates the initials of the craftsman who made it. The cover is suspended by means of a steel cable, with pulleys, to a counter balance weight (50kg). The pulpit is dated 1634 and carries the initials 'G.B.' A roughly made book rest runs around the pulpit and the vanes on the sounding board on the pulpit resemble those on the font cover. The centre pews are also from this same period and are thought to have been produced by local craftsmen. The pew ends are inconsistent; those on the south side crafted in the 17th century are of a 'boiled egg' spherical pattern whereas, the pews on the north side are to a slightly simpler conical or 'acorn' design. In the course of Sir Gilbert

Scott's restoration in 1870, a further variant in pew end design emerges in the side aisles, when the joiners employed, reused as much of the good 17th century wood as possible, using their own initiative to provide a design of their own.

The ancient timber chest at the north door probably dates from the 14th century. This is a fine example of a 'three lock' chest. There is also a Jacobean chest outside the vestry. The High Altar incorporates an altar stone from before the reformation. Nearby are simple 'sedilia' (seats for the priests) and 'piscina' (a bowl in the wall for washing the chalice after Mass), these are from the 13th century.

The east windows were installed in 1914. The middle one has several very unusual features – the 'pelican in her piety' has heraldic crests over the crown; the serpent of evil transfixed into the ground with tent pegs; the sunflower as a symbol of the resurrection.

The pipe organ was built by Mr Abbot of Leeds in 1878 at a cost of around £550. It underwent a renovation in the mid 20th century and is considered one of the finest parish church organs of its size in Yorkshire. The organ was again renovated and overhauled in 1999 at a cost of £15000.

The timber screen in the south east chapel (vestry) was probably constructed from all that Gilbert Scott found remaining of the mediaeval screens across the eastern crossing arch and the two arches to the north and south transepts. The tower contains eight bells, five dating from the 17th century, one being added in 1897 and the remaining two in 1919 as a memorial to those men who had laid down their lives in the Great War.

There is a mediaeval grave cover built into the gable of the east wall of the south chapel. This cover stone may only be seen from outside the church. It is known as a bracelet type with a straight-armed cross superimposed. It would have marked the grave of a knight and without doubt would have originally been inside the church. It dates from the early 13th century and may have adorned the resting place of the Newmarche's.

The heraldic glass in, or hung against some of the windows is mediaeval. It shows the arms of noble families. A number of these families are known to have had connections with Arksey church at various times (unhappily, much of the mediaeval glass has been lost to us due to carelessness or ignorance of workmen who carried out restoration work in the 1850's). Ralph de Nova Mercato, a Norman knight and contemporary of Roger de Busli of Tickhill Castle fame, built his manor house in Bentley in the early part of the 13th century. He assumed the title of Baron Newmarch and held the lands until 1276. When Newmarch fell from grace, Eva Charworth, wife of Robert Tibetot, acquired his possessions.

The Tibetot's two granddaughters married the brothers Roger and Stephen Scrope who held the manor of Bentley, and whose arms, impaled with those of the Tibetot's may be seen in the nave. After the death of Stephen his widow married Sir John Falstolf, K.G. of Castle Coombe. This English gentleman is reputed to be the inspiration of William Shakespeare's Falstaf. His step-son Richard Scrope succeeded him. He too left a widow, who married Sir John Windham of Felbridgge in Norfolk. The Windham family held the lands until 1594, at which point the manor had a succession of owner's right through until February 20th 1636, when they passed to Bryan Cooke Esq., and so began a long association between this famous family and the village of Arksey. Many marks of their patronage may still be seen both in the village and in the church.

In the north transept there is a Cooke memorial that bears the inscription:

"In this tomb rests the body of George Cooke of Wheatley, County of York, Baronet. Who died a bachelor the 16th October 1683 and here waits for resurrection and mercy......."

Opposite the church, Bryan Cooke built a cluster of almshouses in 1660 for accommodating a select few of the poor and needy villagers; he pledged to pay for their upkeep 'ad infinitum'. George Cooke constructed the ancient Grammar School which stands next to the almshouses in

1680, later to become a local authority youth centre and latterly, a Cost-cutter supermarket.

The fine structure at Arksey is Grade 1 listed and is widely described as 'exceptional'. Prayer and praise has been offered here for over 860 years!

In the 13th century a new religious movement reached England. The Friars, who resisted the traditions of existing enclosed orders of monks, and had much more contact with ordinary people and intellectual life. They 'set up shop' in towns to preach to the people and survived by receiving 'alms' to live a simple life. The two main orders of Friars were the Franciscans (followers of St Francis of Assisi, in Italy) and the Dominicans (following the Spaniard, St Dominic). There were male orders (monks) and female orders (nuns). The Franciscan nuns were called 'poor clares'. Similar orders of Friars were the Carmelites and Augustinians.

The Carmelite Friars came to Doncaster in 1346 and in 1350 moved to a site between the High Street and St Sepulchre Gate made available by Richard le Ewere of Doncaster and John Nightbrother of Eyan with patronage by King Richard II and possibly his brother, John of Gaunt. On the six acre site, now in part occupied by the 1740's Mansion House, they created a Priory with a church in honour of St Mary, living accommodation, and an early shrine to 'Our Lady of Doncaster'. The entrance gate was opposite Scot Lane.

The Carmelite Priory was a place of importance on the Great North Road. Passing Royals and pilgrims paid their devotions to 'Our Lady' and lodged with the White friars on the High Street. Here are some of them:

- Henry V in 1399
- Edward IV in 1470
- Henry VII in the late 1480's (journeying north from Nottingham to hear mass before the Lady shrine)
- Henry VII's daughter Margaret on en-route to Scotland to become James IV's Queen.

Given the Priory's dissolution in 1538 no doubt Henry VIII viewed his acquisition while passing through Doncaster to York in 1541 – or at least the prospect of proceeds by sale of land and stone to local gentry. The statue of 'Our Lady' had already been removed by the Archbishop Lee of York and may have found its way to be burnt in London with other Our Lady images.

Bishop Latimer writing to Thomas Cromwell, Henry's chancellor, with reference to the Our Lady of Worcester, says – " She has been the Devils instrument, i fear, to bring many to eternal fire, now she herself with her older sister of Walsingham, her younger sister of Ipswich, and their two sisters of Doncaster and Penrhys, will make a jolly muster in Smithfield. They would not be all day in burning".

Bishop Latimer was himself to burn at the stake along with Bishops Ridley and Cranmer outside Balliol College in Oxford by edict of a new catholic Queen Mary in the 1550's – a brief period of catholic resurgence. Perhaps Doncaster's 'Our Lady' statue still exists in some catholic family Priest's hole? But probably not!

At the Carmelite Priory, 'Our Lady' was surrounded by lit candles and tapers and occasionally devotional gifts. Anthony Lord Rivers penitent's hair shirt after his execution at Pontefract at the end of Edward IV's reign in 1483, Constance Bigod of Settington's silver and gilt work girdle (1449), Katherine Hasting's 'Tawny Gown' (1506), "my best bedes" from Alice West of Ripon and John Twisilton's silver gilt crown. Presumably the bed linen and gown were utilised for vestments.

The Priors were paid by various nobility and gentry to light candles on their behalf at a set number of daily or monthly mass celebrations.

"My Lord useth and accustomyth to paye yorly for the fyndyne of a light of wax to birre befor our ladye in the Whitfrers of my lordis foundation at mastyme dailey"

Just prior to the Henrician dissolution in 1524, William Nicholson of Townsburgh, near Doncaster was fording the Don in an oxcart conveying the Leche family and their household goods. A flood overturned the cart but miraculously all were saved. The Leche wife was swept downstream and they all prayed to Our Lady for her safety — she survived. Hence, a celebration to the miracle at the Priory on St Mary Magdalene's day attended by 300 souls.

Within 15 years 'Our Lady' was gone with no more miracles apparently possible. On November 13th 1538 Prior Stubbis and seven other priors handed over the Priory to the King's Commissioners, Hugh Wirrel and Teshe. The property inventory did not include 'Our Lady' as she had already been removed by Archbishop Lee of York. Given that Robert Aske, the leader of the Pilgrimage of Grace rebellion of 1536, had briefly resided with the Greyfriars in Marshgate, the Carmelites no doubt felt any protest at their dissolution ill advised. The White friars had provided lodgings for the Duke of Norfolk's Royalists despite Prior Cook being a rebel supporter and hence removed in 1537.

Today a new 'Our Lady' shrine, cut from Roche Abbey stone, exists at Doncaster's Roman Catholic St Peter in Chains church in a Shrine Chapel on the north side.

Nothing remains of the original priory and shrine bar the street names and a Pilgrim's Token (Badge) an inch square, now to be found at Lynn museum, Kings Lynn, in Norfolk. The Carmelite Priory at dissolution provided Henry's Exchequer with 11½ lb of plate (silver), land rental for the site, buildings, gardens and orchards of £10 per year, and £23 for the sale of certain buildings. Its marble tomb of Margaret, Countess of Westmoreland, was transferred to St George's Parish church.

Prior Laurence Cook of the Carmelites was imprisoned in the Tower of London from 1538 to 1540 for his support of Robert Aske in 1536. You can still see the name he carved in the first floor of the Beauchamp Tower: "Doctor Cook".

The Franciscan 'Greyfriars' on a 6½ acre Marshgate site, were dissolved at the same time when its Warden, Thomas Kirkham, six friars and three novices were given £3 to divide between them in recompense. The buildings produced 46 tons of lead, four bells and three lb's of plate. The main building sold for £11 plus future sale of the 6½ acre site including four fishponds.

At the dissolution the Crown also confiscated chantry chapel endowments, land, cottage and inn, and sold these including St Mary Magdalene church in the market place to local gentry. The latter site, purchased by Alderman Thomas

Symkinson, was gifted to Doncaster Corporation in 1557 for use as council, court and grammar school premises.

It was during the days of the Norman and Plantagenet kings, from William I in 1066 to the end of Richard II in 1399, that the foundations of modern England were well and truly laid. It was a time of great activity, and the history of this period is full of picturesque romance – of wars and sieges and battles, of intrigue and revolts, of the splendid adventures of the Crusader knights. Churches and cathedrals were built, colleges and schools arose in the towns, monasteries and religious houses dotted the countryside. A great impetus was given to learning. Towns were founded and increased in population. Merchant guilds arose for the protection of trade. Hospitals for sick and poor were built by pious founders. In short, the England of today was very largely shaped by the Norman adventurers and their descendants amongst whom the land had been divided.

It was in those days, as we have seen, that Doncaster was recognised as a town and received its early charters, with a right to have a mayor and corporation. There are several references to Doncaster in that period. It was not a big town, for even in 1379 the assessment of the poll tax, levied on all persons over the age of 15, shows that the population included only 757 persons over that age. In other words, if we put the total population of between 2 and 3 thousand we would probably be well within the mark. The amount paid by Doncaster under this tax was £11 14s 10d. The town had already been represented in Parliament. It seems to have ignored earlier summonses, and it was not until 1337 that it sent 3 burgesses to Westminster. Their names, in modern English, were John Frere, Robert Messingham and John Hedelot. It is worth while recording that, at that time, Members of Parliament were paid – not by the state, but by the town that elected them, the rate of payment being about 2 shillings a day, equal, perhaps, to about £55 of today's money.

Many of the kings of England passed through Doncaster on their way north or south, and it is recorded of Henry III that one night he "slept at Doncaster on his way to York, where he spent the Christmas Holy days". In the same reign, a hospital for sick and leprous people was built, this making 2 within the town. Mary Magdalene church occupied the centre of the town, and the fairs granted in the several charters were held nearby. As the church was in the present market place, it follows that the site has been used for open-air trading for 8 or 9 hundred consecutive years.

Edward II was in Doncaster for a period of 4 days in 1316; and Edward III stayed here at least twice, on his way to and from Scotland, in 1333 and 1336. Before Henry IV came to the throne, when he was Earl of Bolingbroke, he came to Doncaster and stayed at the house of the Carmelite Friars. The visit of Bolingbroke has historic interest, for it gives our town a line in the immortal page of William Shakespeare. Bolingbroke met several nobles at Doncaster. He swore to them that he intended to take possession of the inheritance of his father, John O'Gaunt, which Richard had taken for himself. Later, Bolingbroke seized the crown and had King Richard murdered in Pontefract Castle; and thereupon the barons reminded him how he had falsified the oath he had taken at Doncaster. Shakespeare writes of the incident here:

"You swore to us – And you did swear that oath at Doncaster, that you did nothing purpose 'gainst the state, nor claim no farther than your new fall'n right, the seat of Gaunt, Dukedom of Lancaster." (First pt of King Henry IV, act 5, scene 1)

The town does not seem to have produced any outstanding figure during those times, but very near to it there lived and died a man whose name is engraved deeply into the literary history of our country. Hampole is a little village about 4 miles north-west of Doncaster, and there in a cell lived and died Richard Rolle, the hermit poet and philosopher, whose works are known to every collector of books.

Rolle was a Yorkshireman, born at Thornton, near Pickering. He studied at Oxford, and then, after wandering about the country, he established himself at Hampole, near a Cistercian nunnery. His fame as a writer and the manner of his life as a hermit in a cell, brought him many visitors; and we may be sure that Doncaster was proud of the simple figure of its neighbour, philosopher and recluse.

Rolle's claim to fame is that he was a prolific writer, that he was the first Englishman to use the English language almost solely for his writings, and that one of his works was one of the very earliest books to be both printed in English and actually illustrated as well. It was printed in London in about 1500 by Wynkyn de Worde, the successor to William Caxton, the inventor of printing. Rolle died at Hampole in 1349, so that his book was not printed until about 150 years after his death.

His books and manuscripts are priceless, being preserved in the British Museum and in the Oxford and Cambridge libraries. The first of them, the one printed in about 1500, is entitled Richarde Rolle hermyte of Hampole in his contemplacyons of the drede and love of god – and it is generally known as "Rolle's Contemplations." A literary critic says of him: "The originality and depth of his thought, the truth and tenderness of his feeling, the vigour and eloquence of his prose, the grace and beauty of his verse, everywhere is detected the mark of a great personality, a personality at once powerful, tender, and strange, the like of which perhaps was never seen again."

Another of his works was called The Pricke of Conscience, and this is partially illustrated by an extraordinary 15th century window, in the church of All Saints, North Street, York.

Here we may leave Richard Rolle. He deserves a place on this site because he was a neighbour of Doncaster, and must obviously have visited the town and been known to the town's people. There is no trace of his cell, no clue to his burial place, but somewhere in little Hampole village the emerald green grass grows above the soil where sleeping in peace is this early master of our language.

Chapter 7

Doncaster from Tudors to Stuarts

In the Tudor 16th century the newly enhanced Doncaster corporation developed a wide range of functions with a weekly civil court on Thursdays as a 'Court of Record' (after 1604 with a barrister recorder to keep formal minutes) and a criminal court with its own JP's, sergeants of mace, and ward constable. The Mayor was a coroner and a JP. A Court of Civil Pleas met weekly alongside the JP's magistrate's court, but petty offences could be dealt with at 'Petty Sessions' by the town recorder without a jury. The post of 'recorder' ensured a permanent legal chief executive alongside the elected Mayor, independent of local gentry interests, to record events and enact decisions end-on.

The Tudor Borough Corporation now had a plethora of duties: managing the town's finances; keeping the peace; maintaining the streets, public bridges, toll bars, public gaol, and municipal buildings; sorting out civil disputes; controlling municipal charities; collecting market rights, and dues; and ensuring market organisation.

In 1611 it was renting out 63 market stalls including 25 butchers; 18 shoe makers, 16 wool and linen drapers, and 6 fishmongers. By now the market had an open sided sheltered 'Butter Cross' for country folks to sell their eggs, butter, vegetables, cheese, milk and fruits on market days – a similar, if later (1777), cross remains at Tickhill. Given agricultural changes there was a summer month's wool market whereby wool from South Yorkshire, North Nottinghamshire, and the Lincolnshire Wolds was sold to buyers from the south with up to 6 tons of wool (600 fleeces) being traded in a week. Some of the wool was knitted into stockings by 120 hand knitters in the town, as a household industry to support family incomes, whilst glove makers were utilising the tannery leather with its noxious odours.

By the 15th century the Freemen had been organised into 'companies' (guilds) with their own trading rules. Some guilds still performed annual Corpus Christi pageant 'mystery plays' similar to those whose texts survive at York, Wakefield, and Chester. Tudor guilds in Doncaster of up to 12 members included shoemakers; glovers and skinners (tanners); shearmen; weavers; fulling walkers (wool trade); butchers; 'white' and 'black' smiths; joiners and carpenters; and coopers (barrels). By 1729 the guild tradition remained in only 4 trades: merchants; grocers and haberdashers; tailors and drapers; and blacksmiths. All trading was restricted to freemen except on market days, or on Christmas Eve when locals could offer meat or poultry for sale.

To become a borough freeman was an important social climbing role with a range of benefits and rights to set up as a tradesman, vote at elections of councillors, be eligible for election as a councillor, avoid market or river tolls, vote at parliamentary elections, have sons educated at the new grammar school if desired, and graze cattle on Crimpsall Mede and Low Pasture until the 1880's.

Freemen controlled the borough in the interest of their trading occupations. Freeman status was almost automatic if you were a tradesman or after a seven year apprenticeship to a tradesman, but it could also be purchased and after 1700 'gifted' (by scroll in a silver gilt box in a wooden casket) by the corporation to folk of potential influence or stature. Women were rarely freemen and in the late 17th century Roman Catholics and anti Royalists (not that Doncaster had many of either) were prohibited. There was such a demographic though, as a Catholic gentry family lived at Burghwallis called the Ann(e)'s. DMBC still creates freemen today every six years from public nominations culminating with a Freeman Award Ceremony in the Mansion House with the Town Mayor, in robes, and sergeants of mace present. Recipients receive their scroll in a casket – sadly, they no longer have grazing or voting rights!

By the late 17th century, Doncaster had capitalised on the Great North Road with its colossal increase of travellers. This, added to the Union of Crowns in 1603, meant a revived London to Edinburgh communication. Post 1700 the coaching era brought new passing trade to Newark, Tuxford, Retford, Bawtry (ultimately replacing Blyth), and Doncaster. A Government survey in 1686 identified Doncaster as having guest beds in inns and hostelries for 206; livery stabling for 453 horses; 90 licensed Brewster's; and 100 common alehouses. Many of the latter were simply one room in a house where home-brew was served.

Ale's were also made for Church feasts in mediaeval times and at 'home' breweries on larger estates and at monastic institutions such as Roche Abbey.

Water issues had been part of Doncaster life since Danum days – for Roman bathhouse ablutions; for manorial livestock and domestic needs; for water powered corn mills, essential for creating daily bread; and for navigation on the rivers Don and Idle. Water came from the Don, the Torne, or the Cheswold, or from springs or shallow wells in each village. River water was often polluted by raw sewage and unsafe to drink, hence, it was replaced in the diet by ewes or cow's milk or brewed home ale, as a daily staple for all ages.

It was not until 1694 that the borough contemplated a public water supply through a scheme suggested by one George Sorocold*. Sorocold had become something of a regional expert on water systems using engines (water wheels) and aqueducts. His suggestion involved extracting water from the river Don next to the corn mills, so that it could be transported in lead pipes to a cistern in Hallgate. Gravity would then feed it down hill to the town's houses. John Yarnold turned the concept into a reality in 1697 with a long lease to supply the town's water. It was to be extracted from the river Cheswold at Friars Bridge – a first functional piped supply to freemen's homes or to troughs for washing, and the domestic needs of the lower classes, in an age before Thomas Crapper's water closet. The Cheswold water wheel was still in use in 1830.

The 1690's also brought schemes to improve navigability on the Don to create a 'barge' movement of fleeces and wool, corn, ham's, Cheshire cheeses, Derbyshire lead ingots and millstones. Despite opposition from corn mill water 'leat' owners, landowners fearing flooding of meadows, and a worry for some that Doncaster might no longer be the head of navigation. It was ultimately decided to make the river navigable upstream and improve navigation downstream.

In the 1720's the corporation, in collusion with the Cutlers Company of Sheffield (1624), commissioned a river survey from William Palmer of York. In due course, Parliamentary approval was obtained for a Sheffield scheme from Tinsley to Homestile in Doncaster, and a corporation scheme from

Homestile to Barnby Dun. As a result, the Don was widened, deepened, and straightened to allow passage of 20 ton vessels. By 1830 the corporation was receiving a 10th of its annual income from its shares in 'Dun' navigation – a 50 share scheme with 10 taken by the borough and the rest by 36 freemen and councillors as private individuals. The first, fixed mast, seagoing vessel reached Doncaster in 1848.

A Doncaster clockmaker, Benjamin Huntsman, created a major breakthrough in Sheffield steel making in 1742. Concerned that 'blister' steel was useless in making good watch springs he designed a means of making purer steel using clay crucible furnace pots, which could withstand temperatures up to 1600°c – 'crucible steel'.

Henry VIII's 1530-1540's Church reformation had a major effect on the townscape. Until the 1530's, Doncaster had a typical mediaeval spectrum of religious institutions: the parish church of St. George; a church of St. Mary Magdalene in the Market Place; a Friary outside the town dyke; a 'leper' hospital and chapel at St. James'; a church charity hospice; a Carmelite Priory in extensive grounds off the High Street; and private chantry chapels within the churches. In North Nottinghamshire there were priories at Blyth and Worksop, a small Gilbertine nunnery at Mattersey, and a major monastic centre at Roche Abbey – all of which you can visit to this day. Lord Cromwell and the King's new Court of Augmentation brought ruthless dissolution and an abrupt end to most of the above. Otherwise the buildings and land were confiscated by the Crown and sold to accrue revenues for local gentry and even some wealthy freeholders. A high percentage of the sale proceeds went on Henry VIII's less than successful French Wars. The dissolution sparked a major rebellion of Catholic northern Earls and supporters, hence the Pilgrimage of grace in 1536. Robert Aske rallied Yorkshire support in the East Riding for a rising first initiated in Lincolnshire. He set up a HQ in Pontefract, then moved his large army of like-minded souls to the north bank of the Don at Scawsby Lees. He took up personal residence in the Marshgate Friary. On behalf of the King, the Duke of Norfolk hurried north and camped 5,000 troops in Doncaster and Wheatley and set up 'office' in the Carmelite Priory in the High Street. With the Royalists controlling the bridge, and the Don in flood, no battle took place. Having negotiated Royal promises and a pardon, the rebels dispersed only for Aske and his key supporters to be arrested and executed in York.

Five years later, in 1541, Henry VIII progressed to York via Doncaster to receive due homage from his previously rebellious subjects in the north. By this stage the Crown had taken over the Carmelite buildings (worth £10 in annual rents) plus its 11½ lbs of silver plate; the Greyfriars house in Marshgate with its 46 tons of roof lead, four bells, 31 lbs of silver, together with its 6½ acre site containing four fish ponds; St. Mary Magdalene chantry chapel in the Market place which had acted as a plague house refuge; and 220 acres of other church lands, 47 properties, 5 barns and 2 inns – and that was only in Doncaster!

In 1557, Alderman Symkinson purchased St. Mary's chapel from the Crown for use by the Corporation as a court house and grammar school, although council meetings continued to be held in the 'Moot Hall' next to St. George's church, until 1600.The town had lost the Friar's ability to provide social support for the poor, but Thomas Ellis provided a new plague lodge (hospital) just outside the town and six almshouses in St. Sepulchre Gate plus 71 acres of land and various properties to provide a rent income. The almshouses were rebuilt in 1737 and moved to a site on Goodison Boulevard in the 1960's. Clearly, such benefaction implied a relatively prosperous core of rich freemen and local landowners even if the majority of the population were less than well off.

Doncaster folk remained conservative in religious terms, viewing many aspects of the new Church of England and its puritan reformers with suspicion. In 1612, a survey of 72 parish priests in the Doncaster Deanery identified only five radical puritan clerics. In the English Civil War of the 1640's Doncaster billeted both Royalist and Parliamentarian troops. Thus, in sequence: Charles I was recruiting in town in 1641; Cromwellian infantry under General Fairfax; the Earl of Newcastle's royalist supporters; the Earl of Manchester accepting Tickhill Castle's surrender to Parliamentarians; and then Charles I again briefly in 1641.

From May 1641 to April 1645 some 12,000 soldiers and cavalry were billeted, or camped in, or around the town with inevitably tense problems of theft and disease. Fortunately 100 years were to pass before the next military 'occupation' by a Hanoverian army when 6,000 English soldiers and German mercenaries camped on Wheatley Hills on passage north to counteract the 1745 Jacobite rebellion and it's Stuart 'Young Pretender', Roman Catholic, French supported leader.

Roman Catholics were not to have civil rights in England until the 1830's although Protestant, non-conformist meeting houses (chapels) became legal in the 1689 Toleration Act and developed in Doncaster during the 18th and 19th centuries. To the south, in Scrooby, Babworth, Austerfield, and Gainsborough a more radical Protestantism had manifested in the 17th century and given rise to the Pilgrim Fathers.

* George Sorocold was the engineer that designed the pump for the grand water feature at Sprotbrough Hall.

Chapter 8

Our Streets

*"What a change has come over since we knew it! Our
earliest footsteps were attracted thither by the blossoms of
the fruit trees, beautifully tinted, exquisite in their fair
beauty, rendering it a grove of flowers. Spring indeed was
welcome. We have enjoyed in by-gone years, genial winters
as the ones we have just passed through. Even on Easter
Monday in 1868, the hum of bees, the fascinating colours of
the butterfly, the lark that sky-rocket in feathers, with its
music as it twinkles a mere speck in the clear air of the
sunrise, almost out of sight, but very far from being out of
hearing, we know well what the thing is; it is one of the
morning stars singing for joy – and the jubilant song of
birds were to be seen and heard in the grounds of the
Doncaster Cemetery (Hyde Park Cemetery).
In those vernal seasons of the year, when the air is calm
and pleasant, it were an injury and sullenness against
nature, not to go and see her riches, and partake in her
rejoicings with heaven and earth. What charming walks
were presented, before that great innovator of rural quiet
stretched out its iron limbs (railway tracks). The black and
withered twigs that have worn all the same livery of*

mourning through the dreary months of winter (because there was no skating to be had) are tucking themselves out in their holiday garbs. One is dressed in virgin white, one wears a saffron-coloured robe, another puts on blue, and some twigs somewhere play the dandy in a scarlet uniform. The sunny slopes are reeking with the early mists, and the fields are laying down their carpets for the lambs to dance upon, the sap is stirring in the trees and swelling in the bud, and the breeze comes fresh and fragrant as if it blew through the boudoir of nature while she was getting up in the morning and making a free use of her perfumery. The owl is hooting from the turret, the rook screaming from his swinging nest on the tall elm trees, and the cuckoo shouting from the lonely glen. The blackbird whistles from the bush, and the throstle (thrush) from the grove, and the deep coo of the ring-doves is heard in the woods. The martins and the wrens and the redstarts have come into the concert with small pipes, the nightingale has come with a flute, the linnet and the goldfinch with a lute. Then there are the woodlark and the pipit whose health requires that they should bathe their beaks in music every morning. From the tall hedge or cottage shading tree, the magpie, dressed like a gentleman in black and white, chatters as idly as is usual with gentlemen who are not men. In the heart of the thick wood the jay is screaming. The streams are murmuring through the valley; the trout are leaping in their depths; and cattle lowing on their banks. The bleat of the lamb comes from the meadows. The doors of habitations stand wide open in order to let in the air of heaven. There is eloquence in the wind and a melody in the flowing brooks, like the voice of one beloved singing to you alone.

The primrose we gathered at Hangthwaite (near Scawthorpe), peeping above the wintry mosses, reminding us of the time of the singing birds. Down the long winding lane, over the broad meadow, and on the sunny bank by the wayside, are peeping up, among the emerald grass, the gem-like flowers that were the play things of our childhood – that lured us, years ago, through the dewy dell".

And what about this description of life before and after the Plant Works:

"No argument is required to enforce the high value to a community, situated like that of Doncaster, blessed with the possession of pleasant and convenient outlets from the town, on the score of health and recreation. The main walk across Crimpsall, from the well-known 'Crimpsall Gate', at the termination of Factory Lane, to Isabel Wath, and onwards on the right bank of the Don as far as the cheerful little hamlet of Newton, or from thence to the ancient village of Hexthorpe, had long been held in high estimation. On that delightful open-field footpath, could be enjoyed, at all hours, without let or hindrance, the pure breeze from the west, sweeping down the valley of the Don, without the drawback of dust, smoke, noise, or the least exposure to danger from horses and vehicles. But, 'Crimpsall Gate' is no more. There is also an end to the stroll on the bank of the Cheswold to the old 'Wash', once the favourite resort of the happy angler, and the merry school-boy bather. Gone, too, is the side path on the margin of the old Spansyke Drain in the direction of Hexthorpe Ings; and the drain itself is rendered useless by the construction of the sewers in connection with the Great Northern Railway Plant Works. The path also from 'Crimpsall Gate' across the meadows and by the margin of gardens, called Halifax's Closes, terminating at the junction of Cherry Lane (opposite the Locomotive Buildings), with the Hexthorpe Road and Thief Lane, has shared the same fate; while the Union Workhouse, as seen from a short distance, appears to be stifled by a mass of buildings, as eventually, to threaten its very existence, if it be not bought by the Railway Company, and its inmates transferred to a more suitable locality.

Instead of the once deep green of Crimpsall, even in seasons when other spots were withered with drought, another and less delightful sight now strikes the attention. Early in the morning, with a heavy atmosphere, the long serpent-like trails of dense smoke emitted from the tall engine chimneys of the Plant Works, curl and curve and lay themselves prostrate on the green sward; and it is no unusual thing to see the whole of Sepulchre Gate Without the Bar, or Marsh Gate, enveloped in this fog of smoke".

For the purpose of interest and reference here is a list of Doncaster streets and yards as it appeared in Hatfield's Historical Notices from 1868:

Streets

- Albion Place
- Albert Street
- Alma Terrace
- Arthur Street
- Balby Road
- Baker Street
- Baxter Gate
- Bass Terrace
- Bennitthorpe
- Bond Street
- Bowers Fold
- Bridge Terrace
- Brunswick Street
- Burden Street
- Belgrave Terrace (St James Street)
- Christ Church Terrace
- Camden Street
- Camden Place
- Cambridge Street

- Carr Lane
- Cartwright Street
- Cemetery Road
- Cemetery Terrace (Carr House Lane)
- Cleveland Street
- Church Street
- Corporation Street
- Clifton Terrace (Cemetery Road)
- Dockin Hill
- Duke Street
- East Laith Gate
- Elsworth Street
- French Gate
- Factory Lane (Late Golden Street)
- Fisher Gate (High)
- Fisher Gate (Low)
- Fitzwilliam Street
- Grey Friary Buildings (Marsh Gate)
- High Street
- Hall Gate
- High Street Buildings
- Holmes
- Horse Fair
- Hexthorpe Lane
- Haughton Terrace (Carr House Lane)
- Hyde Park
- John Street
- King Street (East Laith Gate)

- Lawn Road
- Locomotive Buildings (Hexthorpe Lane)
- Marsh Gate
- Magdalenes
- Market Place
- Milton Street
- New Street
- Old Gardens
- Oxford Street
- Pell's Close
- Plant Terrace (St James Street)
- Priory Place
- Printing Office Street
- Portland Place
- Prospect Place
- Princes Street
- Regent Square
- Regent Terrace
- Russell Row
- Sand Pit Lane
- Silver Street
- Scot Lane
- Society Street
- Spring Gardens
- Sunny Bar
- South Parade
- St George Gate
- St Leger Place

- St Peter's Square (West Street)
- St Sepulchre Gate – Within the Bar
- St Sepulchre Gate – Without the Bar
- St James Street
- St James Street North
- St James Street South
- St James Terrace
- St Thomas Street
- Sorsby's Terrace (St James Street)
- St George's Terrace (Marsh Gate)
- Thorne Road
- Whitaker Street
- West Street
- West Laith Gate
- Wood Street
- Victoria Street
- Victoria Place
- Union Street South
- Union Street North
- Young Street

Yards and Courts

High Street -

- Wright's Court
- Harrison's Court

Hall Gate

- Green's Yard

- Bradford Row
- Chapel Yard
- Lightowler's Yard
- Scholes's Yard

Fisher Gate

- Reasbeck's Yard
- Greyhound Yard
- Reed's Yard
- Tattersall's Yard

Cleveland Street

- Marsh's Yard
- Hargreave's Yard
- Holmes Yard

French Gate (West Side)

- Crane's Yard
- Milner's Yard
- Commons Lane
- Priest's Yard
- Mail Coach Yard
- Thackeray's Yard
- Boothman's Yard
- Oxley's Yard

French Gate (East Side)

- Volunteer Yard
- Aldred's Yard
- Reed's Yard
- Burgin's Yard
- King's Yard

- Clarke's Yard
- Church Lane
- Lindley's Yard
- Hallifax's Yard
- Payne's Yard
- Dey's Court

Church Street

- Miller's Yard

St Sepulchre Gate

- Aldred's Yard
- Cade's Yard
- Nag's Head Yard
- Moxon's Yard
- Plumber's Arms Yard
- Booth's Yard
- Ewart's Yard
- Hanson's Yard
- Earnshaw's Yard
- Hopkin's Yard
- Skin Yard
- Crawshaw's Yard
- Black Horse Yard

West Laith Gate

- Alma Place

Spring Gardens

- Chancery Place
- Wesley Place

West Street

- Moore's Place
- St Peter's Square

Marsh Gate

- Tootle's Yard
- Waterloo Row
- Atkinson's Yard
- Palmer's Yard
- Swift's Yard
- Scawthorpe's Yard
- Smirthwaite's Yard
- Naylor's Yard
- Simpson's Yard
- Old Falcon Yard

Baxter Gate

- Wright's Court

Union Street

- Jarratt's Square

Cemetery Road

- Fitter's Terrace

Wheatley Lane (North Side)

- Lockwood's Yard
- Littlewood's Row
- Cheshire Cheese Yard
- Crawshaw's Cottages
- Johnson's Buildings
- Buckley's Row

Printing Office Street

- Drury's Yard

- Hudson's Mews
- Royal Oak Yard

Duke Street

- Jenkinson's Yard

Chapter 9

Social Welfare in Victorian Doncaster

Doncaster's 19th century social reformation remained largely
church, chapel, charity, and GNR driven, be it health care,
education, or poor-law relief. The more affluent made private
arrangements with the medical profession and sent their
children to Victorian boarding schools, or private schools
which sprang up in houses where the original owners had
upgraded to country residences. Thus private education
establishments at one time or another occupied Highfield
House, Beechfield House (1829-41), and Nether Hall (1861-
79). Children of Freemen also had access to Doncaster
Grammar School.

The grammar school lost its old premises with the make-over
of the Market Place in the 1840's to achieve a new market
hall. For the next 20 years it either closed or it occupied a
temporary home, until the Corporation helped fund a
building for 100 students on a Thorne Road site in 1869 –
one large, first-floor, school room with an open (now closed)
arcade underneath, in the best tradition of Victorian Gothic
school room architecture. It was built of local brick and
Ancaster Limestone on a site donated by W.H.Foreman to
the design of George Gilbert Scott. He had recently been the

architect of the rebuilding of St. George's Parish Church in 1858 following the disastrous fire which had largely gutted the mediaeval building. A key figure in driving through the church and grammar school rebuilds and a new infirmary was the Rev. C.J.Vaughan, vicar of Doncaster from 1860 to 1869. He pushed through the plans while he was acting head of a Harrow school. Another Cleric, the Rev. W.Carr Fenton was equally determined so that in 1829 he established the Yorkshire Institute for the Deaf and Dumb in part of Eastfield House, near the race course – a building which previously had functioned as a private race-stand and private school. The school remains on the same site today.

Apart from Mr. Stephen Gibbon's school for 120 working-class children in Spring Gardens, a ragged school, and the workhouse school, the bulk of the towns' children were to be provided with 'elementary' education of a basic function and practical vocational nature from age 6 to 13 in a growing number of voluntary aided school. Initially all of these were C of E aided including that built by the GNR in 1855 at St. James.

The first voluntary school in 1816 was St George's National School. 'National' implied an affiliation to the national society for the instruction of children in the principles of the Church of England. It occupied a site in East Laithe Gate with 250 pupils. As the century progressed further 'National' schools were built including Christ Church on St. James Street (1850's), and The Holmes (1888). The non-conformists and Roman Catholics and Quakers were less than happy that these Church of England schools provided education for their children and were at times fund assisted from compulsory church rates and by Corporation grants. They sought to establish rival 'elementary' schools and the first to open was the Quaker inspired non-denominational 'British' school in Wood Street in 1837 – despite an ultimate roll of 1000 it was over-subscribed.

Forster's Education Act of the 1870's encouraged the building of 'Board' schools governed by local school boards but the Corporation was reluctant to do so although it continued to grant aid to existing schools for building extensions and some running costs. In the 1890's it accepted national pressure and established its first 1000 pupil, non-denominational, free school in Hyde Park thus providing one sixth of the 6000 elementary school places available in 1900. One down side to the new system was the 1902 Education Act which deprived the borough of any control over post-elementary (beyond 14) academic education. This passed to the West Riding County Council only reverting back in 1927 when Doncaster achieved County Borough status. The West Riding took over financial control of the grammar schools and in conjunction with the Borough, built a new academic Municipal High School for girls in 1910.

The borough had a more than laid-back record in Victorian education and hence its school stock, including 7 schools inherited from the Balby and Wheatley School Boards in 1914, was of indifferent quality and was overcrowded. Many of the Victorian and early 20th century school building remain, if not always functioning as primary schools. Of course, given the nature of the British educational compromise many are still Church of England or Roman Catholic in the town and in the villages. A fine example is Carr House Teacher's Centre in the buildings of a towns elementary school.

The borough was equally low key in its involvement in medi-care, but given that in 1850, the 1792 charity dispensary occupied a hemmed-in, noisy site next to the new railway developments, something had to be done. A public appeal for funds was launched in the 1860's to raise £3,500 through bequests and donations, with a Corporation input of £500. In 1865, a new 'infirmary' was built near Waterdale, in a mock-Tudor style, whilst the Corporation used Carr House as an isolation hospital in the event of typhoid, cholera, or TB.

The infirmary now had basic in-patient facilities and, after a further refurbishment in 1903-04 when electricity was installed, it continued in use until 1930 when a new DRI was constructed on its present Thorne Road site. Its out-patients services remained at the old infirmary until 1935. The 1860's building continued in use as Corporation offices and in the last years of the old borough in the 1970's housed it's Education Department, wherein the CEO, Michael Pass, sought to uphold civilised values in an enlarged borough post 1974, involving ex West Riding schools and a fractious social environment with 'Plant' and, in due course, 'Mine' closures. The Royal in D'R'I came about in 1906 when Princess Christian of Denmark, the sister of the then Prince of Wales, became a Royal patron.

In 1834 the Government, alarmed by the cost of Poor Relief, enacted a new Poor Law legislation, amalgamating parishes into Poor Law Unions. Doncaster and Thorne became the central hubs of two such Unions. The Doncaster Union of 1837 covered both the Borough and surrounding parishes with a total population of 32,000. The first Union Workhouse was built in Hexthorpe in 1840 with subsequent enlargement. Only a minority of 'paupers' actually lived in but, by 1870, 250 of all ages did with another 1000 receiving outdoor 'relief'. One third of the residents were children, one third the elderly, and one third able bodied. In 1900, the workhouse (to be renamed the Poor Law Institution in 1913) was moved to a new 30 acre site in what was then largely open country at Springfield, in Springwell Lane at Balby. The new building had a wider range of facilities including: segregated accommodation for males and females, aged, and able bodied classes; cottages in the grounds for elderly married couples; an infirmary; an isolation hospital unit; and a 'lunacy building'. If you wish to experience a time warp to an 18th-19th century workhouse then visit Southall Workhouse (National Trust) in Nottinghamshire. The old 'Springfield House' remains in use in Doncaster for social services purposes.

It was only with the building of the North Bridge over the railway that the Corporation became involved in house provision. The displaced families had to be re-housed by 1913 in 200 new premises on Corporation land in Warmsworth Road, Carr House Road, and Wheatley Lane. The major surge in municipal house building came after the 1925 Housing Act and by the onset of World War II in 1939 some 3,000 houses had been built by extending existing estates and building new ones at Woodfield Road in Balby, and in Intake. By 1974, 'pre-Thatcher', the Council owned a third of all Borough housing: 11,000 houses and flats with new estates in Cantley and Wheatley after 1950.

Chapter 10

Town Sewers in the 1800's

Doncaster in the 18th century, like most towns, gave little regard to what happened to the by products of human existence. The dirt and filth that came from the privy's and washrooms of the community flowed and overflowed onto the crowded streets. Open 'soughs' or drainage channels ran along the side of pavements emitting "powerful" odours and pollution into the very air that was breathed. Not only was the air dangerously polluted but the ground under foot was hazardous to the pedestrian so that accidents were commonplace. Broken limbs, fractured bones, or disfigured faces caused from slips on the raw sewerage became almost a fact of urban life.

Under-drainage, that is to say 'underground' sewers, were unknown to Doncaster before 1802, when on May 5th of that year, plans were ordered to create such systems from 'Wolfindale's corner (Baxter Gate, opposite the News Room) to Dockin Hill, and from Mr. Sherwood's corner (Scot Lane, opposite the Mansion House) to Laith Gate corner'.

On August 28th, 1811, The Corporation ordered "that a public drain of sufficient depth, width, and dimensions, for conveying sewerage from the streets to the river Don shall be properly made and executed from the said river at Dockin Hill to Mr. Morris' shop corner at Sunny Bar in the course of the present year".

The corporation saw fit to have the town's sewers run out into the river beside the water wheel, so that "though we defiled the stream, we actually retained under our nostrils the filth" of which they were supposedly trying to rid themselves. The river Cheswold had become a stagnant cesspool. One man remarked, "The Cheswold would be pure if we would let it alone, and all we have to do is refrain from pouring filth into its waters. On 14th June, 1819, it was unanimously decided by the corporation that Baxter Gate, St. George Gate, and the Shambles (stood in line with the north side of the old market hall), be drained of sewerage. In 1835 it was decided to construct an underground 'sough' (sewer) from Cleveland Street to Duke Street. One author of the time writes, "a circular half-bricked drain 3 feet in diameter from St. Sepulchre Gate, French Gate, and Silver Street was proposed to be made, this work however, was avoided due to its expense. In 1836, Mr. Milner proposed that a drain be constructed to carry sewerage from the top of Hall Gate to the bridge. Again the corporation attempted to dodge the expense stating that it would create a "mammoth financial burden for the taxpayer."

Mr Edward Sheardown suggested that all the wines be sold from the Mansion House cellar to help with the cost but the rest of the corporation wasn't quite ready for such an act of sacrifice, they considered the Mansion House stocks far more important than the health of the towns folk. It was decided later that same year that a compromise was to be reached. They were prepared to start the proceedings by obtaining "estimates for making a common town sewer from Mrs. Vavasour's corner in Hall Gate to the Friar's Bridge, and that such be commenced out of the first available funds of the Town Council."

On July 9th, 1836, a favourable quote was submitted by Mr. Joseph Lockwood and the work was not to exceed £750. The quote went this way:

- "For the 2 ft 6″ culverts at 9s. 10d. per yd. For the 3 ft culverts at 11s. 3d. per yd."

The work was still stalled, waiting for a time when more money was available! The proposals were time and again thwarted by the likes of Sir William Bryan Cooke, Bart. Messrs. Chatham, Dale, Goodwin, Dunwell, Parkinson, Carlton, and Armstrong, until finally in the latter part of 1837 and on into 1838, at a cost of £300. 10s. 10d. French

Gate and Silver Street were drained. After this work the system gained momentum so that in 1839, the main drain was continued as far as Princes Street. Next was the turn of Hall Gate and High Street, which took from the Borough fund, £332. 14s 6d. This was followed by the East Laith Gate sewer.

After still more outbreaks of the Cholera, it was clear that more needed to be done with the town's drainage and sanitation which led to "an effort to rescue St. Sepulchre Gate from its pestilential atmosphere in 1844 as, before this time, the sewer only started from the corner of French Gate and ran to the gaol on Factory Lane. In 1849, Messrs. Charles and Robert Lister undertook for £484. 3s 6d to lay down a sewer along Factory Lane, and St. Sepulchre Gate without-the-bar to St. Thomas Street. In April, 1852, "a 12-inch pipe drain, with two branches, two grates, two traps, and junctions for private drains, was laid at the depth of 12 ft in St. Thomas Street.

Spring Gardens came next at the cost of £44, followed by Cleveland Street, and Marsh Gate. During the construction of the Spring Gardens drain, "an attempt to recover a wooden ten-feet measure, washed down by a heavy fall of rain to the mouth of the main brick sewer, opposite The Good Woman Inn, St. Sepulchre Gate, created fears for the safety of the two individuals, viz. Henry Butterfield and his elder brother

Edward. The hazardous feat was rendered dangerous from the pipes being composed of strong glazed earthenware and only 18 inches in diameter. They were nearly three hours confined in the narrow channel, and just escaped with their lives."

"Printing Office Street and Pell's Close next heard the sound of the Pick-axe and spade. Opposite the Gazette Offices, the pipes were laid at a depth of 15 feet. The ground was found to be treacherous, arising, it is supposed, from the fact of the ancient moat of the Carmelite Friary having an existence close to both thoroughfares. Marsh Gate, or more correctly speaking, 'The Marsh', so productive of boyish recollections for its innumerable dykes and stagnant pools, offering full scope for leaping exercise, was in the autumn drained".

In 1854 came the turn of the top of the town. The drain started near Hall Cross House, along the Horse-Fair, into St. James Street, and terminated opposite the Shakespeare's Head. A new outlet was provided by an arrangement with Mr. Senior, the owner of Sandpit Lock, who permitted the sewage to pass through his land for the sum of £50, "so that it might pass on to the Carr." This whole system cost £1924. 2s. 9d, more than the rest of the town had cost altogether!

By the middle of the 19th century, because of the advancements in the towns approach to sewerage and sanitation, "human life was prolonged from 5 to 50 percent, and house and land property was increased in value by 25 percent! Below is a more comprehensive list of the under-drainage work undertaken by the Corporation during this period:

- 1837-38 ~ Silver Street and French Gate ~ £300.
- 1839 ~ East Laith Gate ~ £90.
- 1840 ~ Hall Gate and High Street ~ £332.
- 1843 ~ Spansyke ~ £53. 13s.
- 1844 ~ French Gate corner to the Gaol ~ £100.
- 1849 ~ Factory Ln and St Sepulchre Gate without-the-bar to St. Thomas Street ~ £484.
- 1852 ~ In St. Thomas Street, 300 ft long 12 inch pipe-drain with two branches, two grates, two traps, and junction for private drains.
- 1852 ~ In Portland Place, 420 ft long 12 inch pipe-drain, with three branches, three grates, three traps, and junctions for private drains.
- 1852 ~ In Cleveland Street, 605 ft long 15 inch pipe-drain, with six branches, six grates, six traps, and junction with private drains.
- 1852 ~ In Spring Gardens, 1072 ft long 18 inch pipe-drain, with eight branches, eight grates, eight traps, and junctions for private drains ~ total cost £290.
- 1853 ~ Printing Office Street and Pell's Close.

- 1853 ~ Marsh Gate to the drain of the Great Northern Railway ~ total cost £175.
- 1854 ~ Hall Cross House, along Horse-Fair, St James' Street, terminating opposite Shakespeare's Head, and to the Carr ~ £1482.
- 1855 ~ St. James' Street, Cemetery Road, Baker Street, and West Street ~ £442
- 1857 ~ High Fisher Gate, Low Fisher Gate (or Friendless Street), and Church Street ~ £378.
- 1858 ~ From Cemetery Gates to Pinfold ~ £34.
- 1861 ~ Water House (North-East corner of Regent Square) to the Low Pasture.
- 1861 ~ Bass Terrace, Lawn Road, and Christ Church Terrace to East Laith Gate ~ total cost £1456. 8s.
- 1862 ~ Regent Square, east and west sides.
- 1862 ~ Pipe-drain from Cheshire Cheese into the River ~ total cost £21.
- 1864-65 ~ The Grand Stand to the Low Pasture ~ £105.

Finally, the link was made between good sanitation and healthy homes. The population of Doncaster began to grow, wealth doubled and quadrupled, every decade has seen fewer funerals in proportion to the living.

At long last, Doncaster "heard more and more merry bells for weddings and christenings."

Chapter 11

Country Seats and Mining Communities

The area west of Doncaster developed a range of colliery settlements from 1850 onwards, linked to the exploitation of Barnsley coal in the exposed and concealed coalfield. They included single terraced rows at the pit gates like Long Row at Carlton near Barnsley; new but largely unplanned small colliery villages; expanded old villages to create colliery towns like Mexborough, Wath, and Wombwell; large new colliery villages away from the pre-existing ones such as Parkgate, near Rotherham; and largely planned colliery villages engulfing existing settlements like Maltby and Denaby, together with those villages that grew up alongside existing ones such as the villages of New Edlington, New Rossington, Bentley New Village, and Woodlands.

Denaby main is a typical colliery settlement built on low-lying Don flood-plain after 1864 – the nearest earlier villages of Mexborough, Old Denaby, and Conisbrough were all a mile or more away. The colliery was to be the deepest and most easterly mine in the South Yorkshire coalfield for 30 years. It reached the Barnsley 9′ 8″ seam at a depth of 448 yards in 1867.

Within 15 years, the Denaby and Dearne valley landscape had radically changed with pit-head gear, steam chimneys, pit works and offices; spoil heaps, tramways, rail sidings, colliery cottage terraces, chapels, a Victorian gothic church, and a school house. A 2nd phase of residential building came in the 1880's as a more planned 'pit village' with a second school, a Co-operative store, and allotment gardens.

In 1889 the Denaby Main Colliery Company came to an agreement to mine at Cadeby under the magnesium limestone outcrop east of Denaby on the Copley estates at Sprotbrough, Cadeby, Scawsby, and Marr Grange. Cadeby colliery opened in 1893 and Denaby township expanded further into Conisbrough parish with 700 houses, three shops, 'management' villas, a Roman Catholic church, another Anglican church, a Wesleyan chapel, and the Denaby Main Hotel, or 'The Drum' as it was known locally, in a 2 phase development next to the South Yorkshire Railway from 1889-93. Around a further 1900 houses were added to Denaby by both the Coal Company and Kilner glassworks bringing the total population to approximately 2500 persons living in 1500 properties. The houses were all built in 2 blocks, one half in the parish of Denaby and the other in that of Conisbrough. They were separated by a 'service' area containing churches, chapels, schools, the Miners Welfare Institute, and eventually, by 1930, a cinema, market place, park, cemetery, and the Fullerton Hospital. Much of the terrace row layout and design was uniform in red brick.

The town was a 'company town' and most of the early miners were not locals. They had no local allegiance to the pre-existing agricultural community. Lose your job, lose your pit house! Hence a tendency for a social split within the workforce between loyal 'company' men and 'union' men.

In the 1960's much of the 100 year old property was rendered obsolete and was redeveloped. Denaby Main Colliery closed in 1968 and Cadeby followed in 1986. The latter site had a brief reprise as the 'Earth Centre'. The Denaby colliery winding wheel still survives as do others at Edlington (Yorkshire Main) and Bentley.

Prior to the age of coal and railways, the Don 'barge' navigation to the west of Doncaster was a landscape of feudal estates and ultimately the landed houses and parks of Tudor and post Tudor country gentry. Tickhill preserves a gentile, country market town atmosphere, with its castle, mill pond, and buttercross, as do parts of old Conisbrough, on the hill with its fine mediaeval castle. To the south west, the tranquillity of the Roche Abbey monastic site as part of the parkland belonging to the Sandbeck estate, contrasts with Maltby's mining township. The Copley estates in and around Sprotbrough, High Melton, and Marr, the Brodsworth House and estate, and Cusworth Hall, recall the properties of local landowners fortunate enough to have mineral rights to exploit.

Bawtry grew as a 'new' market town and river Idle port in the late Middle Ages with a long wide market street on one of the braided stretches of the Great North Road, another of which reached Doncaster via Blyth. The town's plan involved Church street and Wharf street reaching Idle wharfage from the wide Market street. By the late 18th century coaching inns had developed in the form of The Crown in 1780, and The Angel, along with other large Georgian houses. As the head of navigation on the river Idle, Daniel Defoe, visiting on one of his rural rides during the early 18th century, described Bawtry as "the chief centre of exportation in this part of the country, especially for heavy goods, which they bring down hither from the adjacent counties such as lead from the smelting houses of Derbyshire, wrought iron and edge tools of all sorts from the forges of Sheffield, and from the country call'd Hallamshire".

A busy wharfage also exported Derbyshire millstones to Holland, Sherwood Oaks to Medway naval dock-yards, and imported London merchant produce and Baltic softwood timber. All this was lost with Vermuyden's drainage changes, the completion of the Chesterfield canal in the 1770's, and improvements in the Don navigation, cutting out the need for overland carrier wagons and pack horses to Bawtry's wharf.

The Dutch house with its gables (c. 1690) on Church street recalls Bawtry's period as a river and merchant's centre port as does the new west tower of Bawtry church built in 1712 to replace a collapsed tower in 1670 at the beneficence of Samuel Dawson part of an influential local merchant trading family. He resided in the opulent merchant house of 1691 on the market square now functioning as Barton's garage. Further elegant Georgian town houses still front South Parade on the Great North Road south facing the Bawtry Hall estate. The hall was built in 1755 by Pemberton Milnes, a Wakefield woollen cloth merchant, and in the early 19th century it became the residence of the Dowager Viscount Galway thence via Lord Crewe and the Peakes family until occupied as an RAF command centre during World War II and ultimately a headquarters of 'Bomber Command'. It is now Bawtry Hall Conference Centre and a church mission head quarters. Bawtry's mediaeval church is dedicated to St. Nicholas given the maritime trade of the ancient wharfage - a 1930's Ship Inn still exists on the Gainsborough road on the site of an earlier ale house.

The GNR reached Bawtry from Retford by 1849 courtesy of the 'Navvies" employed by the contractors Messr's Peto and Betts. It necessitated a long viaduct, originally a log trestle affair, over the Idle meadows. This was replaced by the current 29 arch brick structure 6 years later to be given cement reinforcement in the 1970's.

The railway resuscitated the town, and the station accrued a wealth of goods facilities: covered goods shed, a grain warehouse, weighbridge, crane facility, and horse stabling. By the 1890's it had 11 shopping trains daily in each direction, including a night mail even though the town's population was a mere 900.

In the 1920's and 30's the station was a hive of activity – town freight traffic, mail bags, signal box, Harworth Colliery coal traffic, coke and tar from the gas works, pick up main line goods trains, Doncaster commuters, and main line travellers. In World War II the Doncaster Rail Control Centre was constructed in the King's Wood cutting complete with concrete roof, blast proof doors, and short wave radio facilities. Royal trains used the Misson branch as a siding for overnight stops in wartime.

The motor age and bus transport helped bring Bawtry's railway age to a standstill in 1968 after 120 years, leaving only the Station Hotel as a reminder.

Tickhill slumbered, post mediaeval, off track from the Great North Road and with its castle redundant and partially demolished in 1645. Parts of the castle survives along with elements of two of the town's mediaeval buildings, namely, the Augustinian Friary which had 8 friars at the dissolution of 1538; St. Leonard's hospital for 'Lepers', re-sited in 1470 and surviving in Northgate as the parish room to the 13th century parish church of St. Mary the Virgin. The 18th Century turnpikes from Balby to Worksop and from Bawtry to Tinsley brought some coaching trade to the 'Red Lion' as the London to Glasgow mail ('Royal Forrester') called here for a period, whilst the 'Scarborough Arms' was used by drovers and the Earl's rent day dinners. The railway age brought the end of droving too. Fairs continued to be held in the market place until the 19th century with a new buttercross being constructed in 1777.

Chapter 12

Hall's of Doncaster

Skellow

Skellow, on the outskirts of Doncaster, takes its name from the river that flows through it. The river Skell flows from its source in Skelbrooke through open country passing through Burghwallis. Shortly before it reaches Skellow Hall it fills the mill ponds of the now redundant Skellow Mill. As it leaves the village, it makes it way for the North Sea via the Ea Beck, Don, Ouse, and Humber.

Skellow Hall, originally built in 1642, would have been a brand new country manor house when Oliver Cromwell came to visit during the Civil War. The Great North Road, now the A1, had to be protected and Cromwell chose Skellow as a base for him to do so. He placed a cannon battery in the village and the mounds that once held the cannon remain to this day. When Cromwell arrived, Skellow would have comprised very little, one or two 15th century cottages would have been opposite the hall and perhaps the reason for him choosing this site would have been the remains of an earlier motte and bailey castle. The bailey is now largely lost under the main road, Cross hill, although some of it does remain in the gardens of Cromwell's Croft and the Cottage. There was reputedly, a 15th century inn here too, now known as 'The Bridge House' but this hasn't yet been confirmed.

There is very little documentation regarding the hall and its residents but what information there is describes a modest but well appointed country house. The hall and outbuildings were constructed using local rubble, the roof was dressed with traditional pan-tiles and the eaves had huge slabs laid to them. The gable ends had coping slabs running down them too. A well known Doncaster magistrate, Captain R. C. Davies-Cooke once lived there.

It started its transition into a children's home in 1949 when £4000 was spent on the transformation. The building is still in existence today, unfortunately the same cannot be said for its big sister, Skellow Grange.

Skellow Grange, once called Newsome Grange, had a concrete render (or stucco) applied to the exterior walls. Miller, the well known 19th century Doncaster historian tells us that it was "the pleasant seat of Godfrey Higgins Esq.", he also adds, "The mansion was built by his father, with this disadvantage, that a piece of land which extended within two or three yards of the south front of the House, belonged to the late George Ann, Esq. of Burghwallis. However, a short

time before his death, Mr Higgins fortunately purchased off him not only this land, but also the manor of Skellow.
On his death, Godfrey Higgins' obituary featured in the Doncaster Gazette on 14th June, 1861 and read:

"Three generations of the family of Higgins have resided at Skellow Grange, the first purchase in the parish having been made by them in 1770 of John Killingbeck, of Clayton. The House has been much improved and the estate undergone considerable change. Skellow Grange and the estate will, we hear, go to Mrs Hatfield, wife of the late Mr Hatfield of Thorp Arch, near Tadcaster."

After this time the House passed from owner to owner, much the same as any modern house would. In later years it was occupied by W. H. Humble, a racehorse owner and then by a Mr Turnbull. The headline from the Doncaster Gazette dated 2nd July, 1964 reads **'Future of Skellow Grange in balance'.** The article then went on to say: **".......... it was recently sold and on Saturday, members of Doncaster Rural District Council were told that the new owner [Mr Turnbull] had applied for permission to demolish it and replace it with a new building. It was decided that the council should inspect the Grange to decide whether or not it is worth preserving for its historical value."**

As seemed to be the order of the day (certainly not to appreciate the local heritage), the Grange was demolished, ending the life of yet another one of Doncaster's fine period houses.

Hickleton Hall

Lord Halifax writes:

"Hickleton village stands almost midway between Doncaster and Barnsley, near the crest of the limestone ridge that surmounts the valley of the Dearne, and in what before the days of colliery development must have been attractive country. The house is a solid eighteenth century building of grey stone with a pediment, to the central block of which had been added on each side a low supporting wing, containing chapel and dining room. As I first remember it, the short drive ran through a grass field, in which the house itself stood, and which after the hay was off was periodically fenced with hurdles for sheep. Shortly after the first was my father converted the field into a formal forecourt with enclosing walls and outer lawns, which certainly gave a great air to the place and set off the standing and stature of the house. But I have never quite lost my nostalgic regret at the disappearance of the field outside the front door, where we used often to hear corncrakes while we did our lessons, and where we had lovely games in the hay, and hounds used occasionally to meet, and where I remember, on a day when old Lord Fitzwilliam had brought his hounds over for an invitation meet, my sister Agnes was kicked off her pony Robin in the full view of the assembled multitude".

".........what I first remembered as the conservatory at Hickleton had been converted into a chapel, in which we attended Matins every morning, with the canticles sung, and Compline on Sunday nights. For many years we had a resident chaplain, and my mother used regularly to play the organ in church, gardeners, footmen, and stable helpers being encouraged to join the choir, for which there was a weekly practice in the House chapel. Every morning we used to repeat to my mother certain allotted texts that we had learnt, and she would give us instruction either on some passage from the Bible, or out of Vernon Staley's book 'The Catholic Religion'............, and it was as much of an excitement for us as it was for anybody else when at Hickleton people turned out from all the cottages with tin cans and drums to drown the oratory of an open air meeting organised by the followers of Mr. Kensit at the time that the Protestant agitation was at its height".

"There has been immense development since those days. Then we all had ponies which, except for bullock carts and hammocks, were the only means of getting about the cobbled roads. Today the bullock cart survives but only as an attraction for the tourist; and the hammock which was the other method employed by ladies for their transport has wholly disappeared. Motor cars are now moving at high speeds up the steepest hills and round the sharpest corners".

"At Hickleton, lawn tennis was never allowed, croquet was; card games in the evening were taboo, but letter games, Halma (similar to draughts) , and chess were all right; for my sisters it was legitimate to knit, but not to sew. We might occasionally be taken for Christmas to Hoar Cross (near Burton upon Trent) or Temple Newsam (near Leeds), but generally this was spent at Hickleton. Here the family year came to be regulated a good deal by the Church seasons and the racing calendar: there might be a short visit to London in February, but the normal thing was to get back to Hickleton for Lent and Easter".

"One of our great interests when we were little was to go into the kitchen and watch the joints being roasted before a huge open fire and having gravy ladled over them by one of the kitchen maids, as the joints revolved on spits by some kind of clockwork. There would be about twenty for dinner and everybody combined to make it look gay. The gardeners came in after tea to do the table, the flowers being chosen so far as might be to match the silver or silver gilt plate; all the plate that could be used was produced; and dinner was a serious affair of six or seven courses – soup, fish, entrée, joint, possibly game, vegetables, sweet, savoury, toast and butter, and dessert; most of it off silver plates on hot water containers which must have weighed a ton to carry up and down from the pantry. People from the village, stables and gardens used to come in and help in the carrying (very necessary as there were two flights of stairs and a long passage from the kitchen) and washing-up; and no doubt ate a good deal that came out of the dining room. There was, I believe, in addition a regular spread in the servants' hall when the work was finished, washed down with plenty of Hickleton beer".

"There were no bathrooms and every guest therefore having cans of hot and cold water carried up to their bedrooms for a hipbath in front of a coal fire, and the bath water emptied with slop-pails; lamps for the sitting rooms and passages when it got dark, taken away by the footmen when the bell was rung to signal that everybody was going to bed, which they did taking one of the silver hand candlesticks set in rows at the foot of the stairs; wicks of lamps and bedroom candlesticks to be trimmed and cleaned next morning; no wonder it had to be a pretty considerable household to cope with it all".

"Quite often there would be a servant's dance, to which each servant was allowed to invite a friend, and fro which in addition there were certain 'corporate' invitations, such as any young persons in the village not otherwise covered, the principal farmers and their wives, Doncaster tradesmen, and a selection of servants from the neighbouring houses. There would be music and dancing, my father dancing with the house-keeper, and my mother with Smith the Butler. There would also be a Hunt Ball at Pontefract and an Infirmary Ball at Doncaster".

Life, in comparison to that of today, was sedate, unhurried, and traditional. Such was the very enjoyable routine of all our Hickleton life. The road from Hickleton to Doncaster mounts a ridge east of Marr through woodland on both sides, and our imagination as children was fed with tales of how in my grandfather's young days on approaching this place in the carriage, the footmen standing behind were accustomed to loosen the pistols in their cases in order to be prepared for attack from highwaymen!

Sprotbrough Hall

(written in 1922)

As it approaches Doncaster the river Don flows between steep wooded banks, on the left side of which, a few miles from the town, stands Sprotbrough Hall. Though the present house was built by Sir Godfrey Copley, the 2nd Baronet, between 1685 and 1690, the site has been inhabited ever since the Saxon 'Sprots' had their home there. From the early 13th century until Tudor times the senior branch of the Fitzwilliam family possessed the place, and many of them are now buried in the adjoining church. Sir John Fitzwilliam of Sprotbrough, who died in 1418 had a considerable family, and from the youngest of his six sons, John, who lived at Milton, are descended the present Earls Fitzwilliam.

When Sir William Fitzwilliam, the descendant of the senior branch of the family died in 1516 he had no direct heirs, and it was eventually decided in the courts that Sprotbrough should go to his aunt, Dorothy Fitzwilliam, the wife of Sir William Copley of Batley, near Halifax. Here, therefore, the Copley's have resided ever since that date. Though failures in the direct line have been frequent, relatives have always been found to succeed, and in one case the heir took the name in lieu of his own. These accidents have had the effect of bringing together a very great number of family portraits of various branches of the family and, among them, portraits of their friends.

Sir Godfrey, the first baronet, procured his title at the Restoration, although he had been a young man and his father dead at the time of the Civil Wars. Another branch of Copley's, however, those of Wadworth, took a prominent part in that struggle, though upon the Parliamentary side, and, on the death of the second Sir Godfrey, the builder of the house, in 1709, it was to this branch that the property descended; these it is to whom we owe the remarkable series of portraits of Presbyterian worthies, which we will deal with after we have considered the interesting gentleman who built the house.

This second Sir Godfrey differed from his father in most respects. The father, though, as we said, a young man of 20 in 1644, yet took no part for King or Parliament, and seems from his later life to have been one of those mild, easy-going people who adorn rather than advance society. His son on the other hand was a man of considerable energy, as was testified by his behaviour on his father's death in 1678, when he was High Sheriff. Sir John Reresby, a Yorkshireman, was the first to hear in London of old Sir Godfreys death; for it was the son who wrote to him, with the pressing request that he should speak to his kinsman, Lord Danby, at that time Lord Treasurer, to get the King to continue the son in that office for the remainder of the year. Says Reresby: *"I was in the house when I received the letter, but went presently to Wallingford House, and found His Lordship had gone to Wimbledon. I was forced to stay to watch his return until 10 at night, and prevailed on His Lordship to go that night to the King lest others should get before us. He found the King at the end of the Long Gallery at the Duchess of Portsmouth's, who presently granted our request, and the patents were made out for the son before it was known that the father was dead. For which trouble I had but a very indifferent return, as the sequel will show."*

Had Sir John been better acquainted with the character of Sir Godfrey, he would have been less prompt to assist him, for Sir Godfrey had all the qualities that make for success in this world. Above all he had an inflexible sense of duty, the duty to himself, which he suffered no consideration of gratitude or family connection to affect. The following year, therefore, which succeeded the confusion of the Popish plot, Copley opposed Reresby in the small borough of Aldborough, which was in the Wentworth interest. Mr Wentworth of Woolley was Copley's brother-in-law, and thus assisted, with the addition of £200 and three lawyers, Sir Godfrey was declared elected, on a recount, by a majority of two votes. In 1681, Sir Godfrey, M.P., married the heiress of a fellow member, Catherine, a daughter of John Purcell, M.P. for Montgomery, by Eleanor his wife, a Vaughan heiress. Thus Copley amassed a considerable fortune, and in 1685 we find him abroad, in Paris, where his eldest son was born. Sir Godfrey, at this time, conceived a taste for French things, and, returning to Sprotbrough on Christmas eve, in time to celebrate his last Christmas in the old house, he forthwith demolished the previous building beyond possibility of discovery, and began the present edifice.

It is improbable that Sir Godfrey was inspired by any particular specimen of French architecture, and the tradition that the house is a copy of a wing at Versailles cannot be corroborated by fact. No doubt Versailles brought home to the Yorkshireman's mind the grandeur of that style, but when he got back to his native county, little more than vague impressions would seem to have remained with him. These, confused in the mind of the Master Mason with English Carolean tradition, combined to produce Sprotbrough. We may, perhaps, attribute to Sir Godfrey's French recollections the segmental arched windows – which are familiar in the ground floor at Hampton Court and in scores of houses built during and after the last decade of the 17th century, but uncommon before 1690, except in isolated examples such as Honnington Hall. Again, the slightly projecting piers in which the windows are set were as yet uncommon in England, while the 2 turrets in the angles of the wings are of French suggestion. Very uncommon are the 2 large area courts between the wings and the main block. A comparison of the north front and the south front will at once show the purpose of the basement for they are built on different levels (a hill). To the north, owing to the slope of the ground, the surface level has been banked up to the horizontal, so that these courts are necessary to light the basement, which itself is necessitated at the south side to give dignity to the upper storey's. There, however, the basement does not form, as is usual in houses of this date built on a slope, a ground floor, but is concealed by a wall and hedge, with the result that the house appears to stand higher than in reality it does from this aspect.

Except for those features, the house is mainly Jacobean. The balustered skyline and the miniature entablature formed by 2 little strap-work scrolls and a piece of masonry above the central windows is reminiscent of pre-Inigo Jones taste. The gate piers on either side of the north front, with the pinnacles that surmount them, are again Jacobean. The excellent simple ironwork of these gates are, however, of more patently French feeling, though it is doubtful whether Sir Godfrey brought back the design. Ornamental ironwork was largely under the influence, at this time, of Frenchmen working in England, such as Tijou, and it is, therefore, more probable that the design was procured in England.

The exterior seems originally, from paintings by Knyff and others, to have been Ashlar in whitish-grey limestone, which is still visible in the rusticated quoins and elsewhere. The greater part of the surface however, had been stuccoed over, probably during the 2nd quarter of the 19th century, at which time all the reception rooms on the south side were redecorated in a plain and ugly manner. The general aspect of the house is not materially altered by this complexion, and, from whatever point it is viewed, presents a stately appearance, with the grace which was the one only importation of Sir Godfrey. The great ornamental importance of the heavy barred windows may have damaged, though not ruined, the scheme by the insertion of windows with thin bars. The effect of this substitution made the building look poor and flat. The broad flight of steps on the Pontack's in Abchurch Street, at that time the only 'French' ordinary in London. In a letter written in 1703, Copley thus speaks of Dr. Hooke: "Your old philosopher is gone at last to try experiments with his ancestors. He is dead and had, they say, only a poor girl with him, who, seeing him ill, went to call somebody, but he was quite gone before they came......., I wonder why he did not choose rather to leave his £12,000 to continue what he had promoted and studied all the days of his life, by that, I mean, mathematical experiments, than to have it go to those he never saw nor cared for. It is rare that virtuosos die rich.

This is a true saying, though Copley himself was among their number, making a very fair collection of second-rate Dutch pictures and first-rate replicas, a great number of engravings, books, and instruments, such as Napier's bones – an early species of calculating machine. Unlike Hooke, moreover, he left a sum to the Royal Society to endow mathematical research, which after some years, produced the fund awarded with the Copley Medal, an honour that is still awarded today. Recipients include Michael Faraday and Charles Darwin.

When Sir Godfrey died of quinsy (a form of tonsillitis) at his house in Red Lion Square off Holborn in 1709, his son was already dead, so that Sprotbrough passed to Lionel Copley of Wadworth, the representative of that branch of the family who had adopted the Presbyterian side in the great rebellion. Commissary-General Lionel Copley, his grandfather, had been in times of peace, an ironmaster. His adventures in politics and war were, on the whole, distinctly unsuccessful. Having at different times suffered imprisonment, whether for embezzlement or treason, in 1649 he was finally incarcerated, after Pride's Purge, when the Presbyterian majority in favour of a settlement with Charles were excluded from the House by the Independent majority. Forty one of the 160 members thus debarred were temporarily committed to an eating house called 'Hell'. Copley, however, with General Richard Brown, Sir William Waller, Sir John Clotworthy and Sir William Lewis, continued in gaol for 5 years without trial. The portraits of these men were painted by the same artist before being hung in the main hall at Sprotbrough. They are fellows with honest, rubicund faces, white lawn collars and black coats. In the top left hand corner of each is a sketch of the White Tower at Windsor, where for a time they were imprisoned, with the years of their languishing beneath. There s a similar series at Weald Hall, Essex, the seat of Mr Christopher Tower, though there, Lewis's picture is missing, while that of General Massy – who escaped at the beginning of the period – is substituted. In addition to the above "imprisonment series", are a very similar, but lacking the Windsor device, of Sir Philip Stapleton, who died at Calais in 1647, and the well known Denzel Holles. Finally there is an excellent portrait of Secretary Thurloe, Cromwell's Chief of Intelligence, a great-granddaughter of whom married a Copley and brought his portrait with her.

The principal Copley achievement in the field was the winning by Colonel Christopher Copley, Lionel's brother, of the small battle of Sherburn, which, however, was of great value to the Parliament, as resulting in the capture of Charles' confidential and extremely compromising correspondence with Lord Digby in the matter of raising the Irish Catholics, and the occasion of the impeachment of Stafford in 1640 had been a phrase in a letter to Charles which was constructed to refer to raising an Irish force for service in England. We mention this in passing as there are 2 portraits of Stafford at Sprotbrough – one a Van Dyck, showing the statesman caressing a greyhound, similar too, but in better condition, than the one at Wentworth; the other shows him with his secretary, an engraving of it is appended to his "Letters."

The Lionel Copley who succeeded Sir Godfrey died at Bath without heirs in 1719, and Sprotbrough went to a son of one of Sir Godfrey's daughters – Joseph Moyle of Bake in Cornwall, who adopted the name of Copley and was created a baronet in 1778. His second son, Sir Joseph, was mixed up with the old scandal of the Earl of Abercorn at the end of that century. The Earl had married a Miss Copley for his first wife, whom, since she had poor health, he more or less ignored. On her death, having for some time been in love with his cousin, a Parson's daughter, Cecil Hamilton, he persuaded Pitt to get the King to confer a title on her that he, the Earl, might marry her without injuring his family pride. The plan was carried out, but they were not happy, and the lady was subsequently divorced and married Sir Joseph Copley, her predecessor's brother. The daughters resulting from this union were famous and witty young ladies in the years succeeding Waterloo, and, known as "Coppy" and Maria, corresponded with naughty old "Creevy" and were the somewhat unapproachable queens of the Radical Kingdom.

'Coppy', the more brilliant of the two, died unmarried in 1887, while Maria married Lord Howick, son of Lord Grey of the Reform Bill. When their brother died in 1883 the house again went to collateral, Sir Charles Watson, who added the name of Copley to his own, and whose daughter, Lady Copley, is the present representative of the long line which most cursorily we have surveyed.

The family history is remarkably well illustrated by a mass of family portraits, though, by their copiousness many are hard to identify. In the hall, however, we see Sir Godfrey, M.P.,F.R.S., above the boldly moulded chimneypiece, painted by Kneller. This hall and the entrance hall next to it are practically the only rooms in the house that have not been redecorated. At the eastern end of the former there is a charming derivative of the medieval and Tudor screen, in the form of an arch flanked by two flat topped doorways, which gives on to the stairs. The carving is very restrained and fine, and two diminutive spandrels, containing cupids' heads occupy the spaces above the arch, while panels with broken corners surmount the two doors. A set of five excellent walnut-veneered chairs (two with arms), are present. They are an early example of the type of chair associated with the name of Chippendale, from which the shaped splat, and flat cross piece at the top, familiar in Queen Anne chairs, has not yet quite disappeared. At the opposite end of the hall hangs the Stafford Van Dyck, above a Nonesuch chest in excellent preservation, with the original tinned hinges and a hanging box inside.

Sir Godfrey is recorded to have paid £150 to Henry Cooke to undertake the internal decorations. All of this artist's work, which is pointed out as such, are some rough chalk portrait sketches, but it is fairly certain that he painted the ceiling in a little boudoir, marked in the plan. Cooke was employed at Hampton Court on the Cartoons of Raphael, which he is said to have executed in turpentine, a manner of his own. This was probably a kind of 'thin oil' painting, and the ceiling in question is not very striking, whether for colour or design, in that the greater part is a blank, with the heads and shoulders alone of the deities who should have filled it showing as though peering over the cornice. If Cooke did any more work, and it is probable that he did, none remains, though it is possible that some of the ceilings now whitewashed were originally covered by his design. The rooms on the south front, as we mentioned above, were redecorated during the early 19th century, at a time, the only time, when the house was let and not in the occupation of the owners.Sprotbrough Hall and estates were sold off in 161 lots at the Doncaster Guildhall in September 1925. Earlier, a number of tenants had bought their holdings by private treaty. F.S.Gowland of Ripon, bought the hall along with 115 acres of the estate for £9100. By 1926 the hall was being demolished to make way for new development. Reputedly, the hall was knocked inwards using the rubble to fill the cellars up to ground level, the excess stone was used as the foundations for the houses on Brompton Road. So, if you live on the Park Drive estate in Sprotbrough, and your spade hits something hard in the ground, you may just have found a little piece of the Copley's grand country seat!

Chapter 13

The Corporation and Mansion House

The 18th Century saw great movements throughout the land. The rise of nonconformity and its spreading influence, the growing power of Parliament, the increased attention paid to the education and comfort of the people, the development of trade and industry – all these things are reflected in the life of the town.

By now, Doncaster had settled down into the character it possessed until our own time. Full rights of self-government ere centred in the Corporation. The old feudal days had gone forever. There was no lord of the manor to collect tolls and dues and have his say in the regulation of the town's affairs. The de Mauley's had passed away. One of their successors, a Salvin, brought an action against the Corporation to have it established that he was overlord of the town and owner of the manors administered by the Corporation but the Corporation practically bought him out by a payment of something like £3,000, and, in return, Salvin executed a deed in which he renounced all claim on the lands and estates of the Corporation.

From that date there was no more disputation on that subject, and the Town Council was free to collect its dues, to spend them as it liked, and to pass its own laws for the government of the town. Writers of history call them "the good old times", in a sense, they were. The modern manufacturing towns had not grown to their present dimensions. Factory acts were unknown. Life was more placid than it is now, not so feverish. There was no telegraph and no telephone; no steamship and no railway engine; and certainly no aeroplane and no motorcar.

But the "good old times" had their drawbacks. Education was outside the reach of the poor, there was a great deal of poverty. None of the comforts and amenities of modern civilisation had been introduced. There was no scheme of water supply, no lighting service, no sanitary institutions, no medical officers of health; people were thrown into prison for very small offenses, they were hanged for sheep-stealing; the towns were dirty and ill paved, and the country roads were infested with highwaymen.

To see how Doncaster, in common with other towns, emerged from this state of things and travelled, even if slowly, along the path that has brought us to our present perfection, is interesting.

The Corporation in the 18th century had great revenues. It still possesses remarkably rich and ample estates at Sandall, Wheatley, Balby and elsewhere, bringing in great revenues. But in the 18th century, these estates were much larger, and it is a thousand pities that the ancient manor of Rossington, which had been in the possession of the town for centuries, should have been sold in the early part of the 19th century, by a town council which thought more of the pleasures of life than of the possibilities which the ownership of such an estate possessed for future citizens. We may be sure that no modern town council would thus so lightly part with lands it had so strenuously fought to preserve against the legal attacks of wealthy landlords.

But in this matter Doncaster Corporation would only be on par with other towns. It built a handsome Mansion House as the centre of the civic life of the community, and for that wise action we can forgive much. As far back as 1771 it passed a resolution that the Mayor should wear a scarlet gown trimmed with fur, and also a gold chain with a medal (with the Corporations arms on the one side and the Kings arms on the other), and we have seen that the Aldermen and councillors were robed only a little less magnificently. The civic pageants were gorgeous. The Corporation turned out in full splendour on the smallest excuse. Processions through the streets were regular sights. The old Town Hall in the Market Place was out of date, and the Corporation were ambitious to house themselves in a more fitting establishment. Hence, the Mansion House – the imposing building in High Street which is still one of the great architectural features of Doncaster. It was begun in the reign of George II, and the curious may like to know that the London Mansion House was also erected in the same reign – in fact, there are only 2 years or so difference between erection of both these buildings.

It has been long a boast of Doncaster that it has one of the only three Mansion Houses in England, the other 2 being at London and at York. Thus Yorkshire had the distinction of containing the only Mansion Houses in England outside London.

Now, a Mansion House is what the name suggests. It is a Mansion, and it is to provide the Mayor with an official residence. Mayors of Doncaster for generations lived at the Mansion House. There was a staff of servants, there was a cellar – always well stocked with wine. Noblemen sent venison and game for civic banquets. Dinners, Balls and assemblies were of frequent occurrence. Ever since it was built, our Mansion House has been a centre of hospitality and gaiety, and a mere list of the entertainments it has provided, and the distinguished visitors who have dined and danced in its beautiful saloons, would be quite imposing. Nowadays, Mayors no longer use it as an official residence.

The Mayor has a private parlour which he uses for his correspondence, for receiving deputations, and so on. Corporation banquets and balls are of frequent occurrence during the winter. Meetings, bazaars, charity functions are held there by public bodies with the consent of the Mayor. Civic processions always assemble there and make a start from the steps that lead down from the massive door. Proclamations, such as election results, etc., are usually read to the town's people from these same steps, and during the war, the Mayor and Corporation many times stood upon them and reviewed the troops that were in training in the town.

It was in 1744 that the Corporation ordered plans to be drawn up for the building of a Mansion House, and in the same year it was ordered that the work should start. The money to pay for it was borrowed on bonds. It was ready for occupation in 1750. Its cost was recorded at the then considerable figure of £4,500, but at the time of the Municipal Reform Act in 1835 it was stated that the Mansion House, by then had cost the town £12,000, taking into account alterations, furnishing, beautifying, etc.

Not all the costs came out of the pockets of the town. For many years it was the custom for the aldermen to pay 15 guineas to the Mansion House "in Lieu of his customary feast", and the sum was usually spent on plate, china, linen, furnishings, and so forth; and that is one of the reasons why the collection of plate and furniture is now so valuable and complete.

In fact, the Mansion House collection of insignia, silver-plate, cutlery, epergnes, bowls, candlesticks, etc., is probably unique so far as regards a civic collection in the provinces. The maces and chain which form a part of the mayoral equipment are extremely old. Doncaster was given the right to have two sergeants-at-mace in Edward IV's charter of 1467, and the sergeants still form part of civic processions, carrying silver staves or wands. How old these are we do not know, but by resolution of the town council in 1759 they were ordered to "be made new", signifying, surely, that they were then wearing out through usage. That date fixes them as having been in constant use for the last 161 years, and how much older than that they are we dare not even guess. They bear the Royal Arms before the union with Ireland.
In the case of the mace, a massive piece of silver-gilt, we have its full history. It was presented to the Corporation by Sir George Cooke, the first Baronet, of Wheatley Hall in 1683. According to the records it cost £70. It bears the following inscription:

"Ex dono Georgii Cooke de Wheatley in com. Ebor, Baronetti, 1683". When translated this reads, *"Given by George Cooke of Wheatley, County York, Baronet, 1683"*.

It also bears the Royal motto:

"Honi soit qui mal y pense".

On receiving it, the Corporation appointed a mace-bearer at a salary of "four marks per annum", the first office bearer being one Richard Brigham. It is believed that this mace is one of the very oldest Corporation maces in England. If any other Corporation owns one with a date earlier than 1683, they are to be envied.

The Mayor's chain is not so ancient, but it boasts a long record. By resolution on 11th September, 1771, the council " ordered that a scarlet gown trim'd with furr, and also a gold chain with a medal with the Corporation Arms on one side, and the Kings Arms on the other, shall be had for the use of the Mayor for the time being". On New Year's Day, 1772, the chain was ordered at a cost of £69 5s.

The Mansion House contains a ballroom, banqueting room, reception room, and saloon. Its outside frontage is quite imposing, and its interior, in the spaciousness of its noble apartments and the beauty of their decorative scheme, makes it a very valuable ornament of the town. On the walls are full-length portraits of Queen Victoria, George II, the Marquis of Rockingham, Earl Fitzwilliam, Sir William Bryan Cooke (first Mayor after the reform act of 1835), the Rev. Dr.

Vaughan (a celebrated vicar of Doncaster, afterwards known as Dean Vaughan), Sir Frank Lockwood (an eminent Q.C. and M.P. of Victorian days, who was born in Doncaster), and one or two others. The corporation plate, which is signed for by each Mayor on his accession and is formally handed over to his successor at the close of his year of office, is kept in a strong room.

Other corporation buildings may be noted. The Guildhall, in Frenchgate, was erected in 1847. This was the building which in other places would have been known as the town hall. The police offices and cells were there. A large public hall was provided for dances and meetings. The County Court and the Borough Police Court are held in a special courtroom below. The Town Council used to meet there; but when the borough was enlarged in 1914, and additional members were brought into the council, the room set aside for their meetings was not large enough, and so the whole body moved across to the Mansion House.

Doncaster has been a market town for centuries. Markets and fairs were mentioned in some of the earliest charters granted by the Norman Kings. The tolls were originally claimed by the Lords of the Manor, but in time they reverted to the corporation and for many hundred years they have been a source of revenue for the town. The old mills on the river, which also paid revenues, which also paid revenues, have all gone, but the markets are more important than ever and the scene on a Tuesday, when cattle are brought in from miles around and sold at auction, and on a Saturday when the country-folk display their products of farm and field and orchard, proves the commercial importance of this aspect of local life.

The market hall occupies the site of the old Town Hall and St. Mary Magdalene's church. It was built in 1847 and was enlarged in 1871, when the corn exchange was added to it.

The corn-exchange was the largest public building in Doncaster. In addition to serving as a corn market on Saturdays, it was used for concerts and public meetings and many of the stars of the operatic world appeared upon its platform.

Chapter 14

Doncaster Military

Doncaster has a military history of no mean note, and there are on record several instances where the Government has thanked Doncaster for services at home and abroad. At present the town is the headquarters of two auxiliary regiments, viz., The Queens own Yorkshire Dragoons Imperial Yeomanry and the 2nd V.B. York and Lancaster Regiment, and it is only by the merest chance that a garrison has not been established here, for negotiations to that end were in progress some years ago, but the objection of the corporation saw Pontefract secure the choice.

To take the Yorkshire Dragoons first, this being the older regiment of the two associated with Doncaster, according to a booklet issued in 1893 by Mayor Somerville, of the Doncaster Volunteers, and from a pamphlet written for the Army and Navy Gazette in 1898 by Sergeant-Major Leach, of the Dragoons, the Dragoons were instituted in 1794 at a meeting at Pontefract, over which the Duke of Norfolk presided. A meeting to co-operate was held in Doncaster in May of that year when the corporation subscribed £525. Two regiments were formed; the first, or southern regiment, consisted of three troops for Strafforth and Tickhill, one for Doncaster, two for Rotherham and Sheffield, one for Barnsley and two for Pontefract. The second regiment consisted of five troops, the Earl Fitzwilliam being Colonel-commandant of the whole corps.

In 1796 as an intention was manifested of making descent on this kingdom, a levy of 15000 men from the parishes was made, and to this number, Doncaster contributed its quota. The title of the regiment at this period was the Southern Regiment, West Riding Yeomanry Cavalry. In January 1795, the thanks of the magistrates were given to the Rotherham and Barnsley troops for their readiness in assisting the civil power at Wath.

On November the 8th, 1796, three standards were presented to the regiment – the Royal Standard, given by the Doncaster Corporation; the second, or provincial standard, bearing the arms of York, by Earl Fitzwilliam and the third by the ladies of Rotherham. The regiment was mustered for 14 days' training at Leeds in June, 1799, and attended drills in 1800 and 1801. In April 1802, orders were received for the disembodiment of the regiment, but on July 11th 1803, at a meeting convened by the Lord Lieutenant, it was resolved to raise it again. The accepted strength of the regiment was then 612, exclusive of officers, Lieutenant-colonel Foljambe in command. Considerable zeal was manifested, and the yeoman expressed their willingness to serve in any part of the kingdom. An opportunity for assembly was given on August 15th 1805, when the Woolley beacon was set ablaze by mistake, and 3500 yeoman and volunteers were set in motion before the mistake was discovered. The Southern Regiment (Yorkshire Dragoons) had the creditable muster of 301 out of 342 on this occasion. In 1806 the regiment was reviewed by the Prince of Wales. In 1840-2 the regiment did considerable service in the suppression of the Chartists riots for which it received the thanks of the Commander in Chief. In 1844 the designation of the regiment was changed to the First West Yorkshire Yeomanry Cavalry, and on August 27th 1851, four troops with the band had the honour of escorting Her Majesty on the occasion of her visit to Doncaster.

In 1871, the regiment as organised in 1803 ceased to exist, and the corps was formed of the following eight troops:

- A. Sheffield
- B. Kiveton Park
- C. Doncaster
- D. Barnsdale
- E. Wentworth Park
- F. Pontefract
- G. Barnsley
- H. Wakefield

On the death of Lord Wharncliffe, December 19th, 1845, the command was taken over by the Viscount Milton, who became Earl Fitzwilliam in 1857. In 1887 Major the Hon. C. W. Fitzwilliam was gazetted to the command in succession to Earl Fitzwilliam. The present commanding officer, Colonel the Earl of Scarbrough, has seen nearly thirty years service, including seven in the 7th Hussars. He was promoted to the command in 1891.

During recent years the regiment has had the distinction of being inspected by the Duke of Cambridge and Viscount Wolseley, while in May, 1897, the Sheffield squadron had the honour of escorting Her Majesty at Sheffield, and the regiment was represented at the royal celebration of the year. The title of "Queens Own" was conferred in 1897. For many years the regiment assembled annually for training in Doncaster, when the men were billeted in the town; when the brigade system came into vogue, the regiment was away often. This system lapsing, the regiment again returned to Doncaster, but this time for encampment, the scene of the camp being the race common, and the period of encampment, 16 days. This year (1903), the regiment will assemble at Wellbeck. The present strength is 640.

The recent war in South Africa gave volunteers the chance that they had long looked for, and during the time following the call for volunteers Doncaster was the scene of much military activity. All the Yorkshire Yeomanry with the exception of the first contingent being raised and equipped here. The Yorkshire Dragoons sent out 100 men and altogether no less a number than 1,702 men were sent out in the Yorkshire Imperial Yeomanry. All but the first contingent of about 300 were recruited and equipped in Doncaster. The officers who went on active service were the Colonel (The Earl of Scarbrough), Major Simpson, Major Brookes, Captain Smith, Lieutenant Jeffcock and Lieutenant Brooks. A number of men who hadn't previously belonged to the corps and who saw active service in South Africa have recently joined, so that the regiment, as well as having the distinction of being one of the strongest yeomanry regiments in the country, must be very hard to beat in the direction of active service members.

Chapter 15

Doncaster's Brave Volunteers

It was in August 1806 that the first serious steps were taken in the direction of forming a corps of volunteer infantry in Doncaster. More than £1000 was collected and to this sum the corporation contributed £400. The men were allowed by Government, twenty shillings each for clothing and one shilling per day when on permanent duty. The regiment was 500 strong, to which number the town contributed 200. It was under the command of Lieutenant-colonel Commandant William Wrightson, Lt. Col. Sir George Cooke – Bart, and Major Samuel Clowes. The Doncaster companies were officered by Captains Leonard Wallbank Childers, James Jackson and Thomas Rimmington all of whose names are honoured in Doncaster's History. 3000 stand of arms and 31000 cartridges were sent to Doncaster for the infantry of the district.

On the 11th May of the following year, two splendid colours, after having been consecrated by the Rev. W. Childers, the chaplain, were presented to the volunteers by the Mayoress (Mrs Jackson). On the following day the regiment marched to Pontefract for fourteen days training and at various subsequent periods the assembled for training. On the occasion of a false alarm at Woolley Beacon (the beacon was set ablaze by mistake), the Doncaster infantry mustered 341, only 45 being absent. In July of 1806 when Napoleons preparations for invasion were being carried out, the Doncaster Volunteers were assembled, when out of 500 men, 11 officers, 10 sergeant, 5 corporals, 4 drummers and 129 privates volunteered for service with the militia, and many other joined up to October in the same year. At the peace of 1814, the volunteers were disbanded.

With the formation of rifle corps, Doncaster came into line in 1860, a company being formed of the operatives and others employed in the works of the Great Northern Railway, officered by the some of the officials of the company. A second company was raised amongst the burgesses and others of the neighbourhood. The 2nd V.B. York and Lancaster's are one of the strongest single battalions in the whole of the volunteer forces and out of about 30,000 troops mustered on Salisbury Plains last year were actually the strongest. From a table of figures prepared by regimental Sergeant-Major Richardson, we find that last year the regiment was 1,144 strong. The regiment comprises 10 companies, of which 5, counting the cyclists one, are at Doncaster. The cyclist company was formed in 1890 by Major Somerville. The regiment forms part of the South Yorkshire Brigade, which includes also the Hallamshire Rifles (1st V.B.York and Lancaster regiment) and the Kings

Own Yorkshire Light Infantry (Wakefield). The battalion had the misfortune to lose the most popular officer in Colonel Johnson (Wath) in January. Colonel Stoddart (Rotherham), who has been with the regiment ever since his youth, is the present commanding officer, and one cannot speak of the Doncaster volunteers without mentioning Colonel Elwis, recently retired, who went through every grade, commencing as a private. Few, if any, volunteers' regiments at all, responded more heartily to the call for volunteers in the recent war, than did the 2nd V.B.York and Lancaster. Sixty eight men picked out of far beyond that number of those who offered, went to South Africa in February of 1900; a further picked lot, said by those who are authorities on the point to have been one of the finest bodies of infantry physically, that one could look upon, 59 in number, went to South Africa in 1901, and in 1902, eight more were sent out. The officers who served at the front were Captain Boyle, Captain Moxon, Captain Longden and Captain Barnes, while 2 or 3 others went out apart from the York and Lancaster's. Apart from this, the regiment contributed no less than 107 men to the active service Imperial Yeomanry, so that in all, out of about 1150 men, the regiment sent 242 men to the front, while during the war 53 joined the regular army.

Butts, for shooting practice, were erected in October 1860 in the plantation on the east side of the running course of the Race-ground. They are built of brick, 75 feet long by 30 high, topped with stone with strong buttresses at the back. The targets are of iron. The cost of the butts and targets was £210. The regiment showed quite the proper spirit during the emergency camp of 1900, when out of 1103 men, 1036 attended for training, 556 staying during the whole of the month. The regiment will go into brigade camp at Scarborough in July of the present year.

As a memorial of the late Queen Victoria's Jubilee, the officers of the local volunteers set on foot a movement for the provision of a suitable drill hall, the accommodation up to that date being very mean – practically nothing more or less than a few back premises and a yard. The drill hall cost about £2000. It is situate in Frenchgate, and stands back from the road. The hall is well appointed, there being officers', clerical, and other departments, and a splendid drill room, spacious enough for two or three hundred men to be put through manual and physical exercises.

The 3rd Battalion York and Lancaster Regiment (Militia) is most closely associated with Doncaster, the regiments colloquial title being the Doncaster Militia. The regiment camped here for annual training for many years, and a revival of old times was witnessed the year before the South African outbreak, when the battalion was encamped on the Racecourse for six weeks. The Doncaster Militia served in the South African War, and its Colonel, a brave Christian soldier, beloved by his men, and who was in command during the encampment at Doncaster, laid down his life for his country.

Chapter 16

Doncaster and the Great War

Like all other towns, Doncaster was immediately drawn into the vortex of the Great War. This website, with its narrative of the outstanding features of the town's history, would be incomplete if it failed to place on record some account of the part we played during the tragic years from 1914 to 1919 – when the shadow of a mighty conflict hung like a shadow over the land, and the heart of the nation was stirred to its depths at the immensity of the task to which we had been called.

This is not meant, of course, to be a history of the war. We are here not concerned with the story of the titanic struggle "over yonder" – the din of battle in France and Flanders, the ebb and flow of victory, the dark days of depression, relieved by the glowing heroism of our men, with all the splendour of their vivid achievement. We do not carry the reader to the Retreat from Mons, nor to the Battle of the Marne, nor to the deathly struggle before Ypres, nor to the great days of the final offensive that broke down the German rush and caused the Kaiser to flee like a criminal and his armies to throw up the sponge. Nor is it for this simple book to tell the epic story of the Navy, nor the thrilling romance of our Eastern victories. We confine ourselves to the recital of the share, the great share that Doncaster took in the campaign, leaving the wider canvas to the pen of the better qualified historian.

In the years to come the story will be read with even deeper interest than it possesses now, it begins on 4th August, 1914, when the drums of war rolled out their booming message; when our local Territorial Battalion, the 5th King's Own Yorkshire Light Infantry, was recalled from its holiday camp at the seaside and placed upon a war footing. And what a panorama lies between that date and the present! We look back to that famous Bank Holiday, when war was declared – when we stood at street corners and saw the "boys" in khaki rushing to their appointed stations. We saw the 5th coming into the town, then the Yorkshire Dragoons, spic and span in accoutrement and equipment, followed by the West Riding and other regiments. Doncaster people still remember the tramp of armed men through the streets, the billeting of soldiers in our homes – the first time in living memory – the bivouacking of soldiers in the open space before the Market, and the wide-eyed wonder of the townsfolk as they saw rifles stacked and the military cooking their meals in the open beneath the August sun.

War had come, and the whole face of the land was transformed. Men were enlisted by the thousand. New battalions were created. First a company and then a full division of Royal Engineers were recruited in the town and neighbourhood by the Mayor and a committee, at the request of the War Office. Train loads of newly-made soldiers left the town. Military hospitals were opened by private enterprise – the Arnold, the St. George's, the Loversall, the Hooton Pagnell, and others. Relief committees were formed. A new Volunteer movement was started. A Rifle Club was founded. Special constables leaped into activity. And as the war progressed, Belgian refugees – poor souls hunted and harried form the hearth and home – came to Doncaster to find the peace and shelter denied them by the invading foe. Local manufacturing establishments abandoned peace work and responded to the Army's call for munitions. Thousands of women entered the works. And as the demand for men for the Army increased, the women took their places in civil life. Women Tram drivers, women postmen, women window cleaners, women bank clerks, women land workers – there was hardly a sphere of human activity in which the women were not found – that the nation might carry on, that the men might be set free for the greater and harder work of keeping the Hun from placing his feet on our inviolate soil. Nearly every manufacturing establishment in the town, headed by the Plant Railway Works, began making munitions. The Race Common was the site of an aerodrome, where thousands of young men learned the art of flying machines.

So the story moved on. We saw the opening of clubs and institutes for the soldiers in the town - the raising of money for comforts for the troops, the sending out of Christmas gifts, the enlargement of the military hospitals, the hundred and one movements which sprang into being for no other purpose than that of helping the nation to win the war and to beat down the tyranny of the German foe. How many hundred thousand pounds did Doncaster raise for war purposes? The full total will never be told. But it is a fact that the town and district furnished the state with over a million and a quarter in an answer to its appeal for subscription to War Loans. No appeal went unanswered. The heart of the town was stirred, and its hand was ever open. We hardly knew what it was to have the luxury of even an occasional Saturday without a "flag day".

Meanwhile we at home, just like those at the Front, were undergoing our own dangers. The Zeppelins roamed the midnight sky, and their murdering bombs fell upon defenceless people. Happily, we in Doncaster came out unscathed. Not a bomb fell upon our town. Not a life was lost. Yet it is curious that within a radius of 18 miles from Doncaster, German airships wrought terrible havoc at Sheffield, Goole, Retford and other places. Privations of another sort, though small in comparison with those our defenders experienced, fell to our lot. No lights were permissible which might serve as a guide to the enemy in the skies. Our public street lighting was abolished. Our houses and shops were veiled in darkness. Not a gleam of light was allowed to penetrate into the street. We went about at night in deepest gloom. Railway trains and tram cars were shrouded. Motor car headlights were forbidden. Even the lamp of the humble bicycle had to be reduced in power. As petrol became scarce, motor cars were forbidden, except on public business. Food became scarce and a hundred and one restrictions were imposed. White flour gave way to brown. The delicacies in the sweet shops and confectioners were swept away. Finally, food was rationed, and from the Food Office in High Street all of us had our ration cards and lived on a scientifically-based allowance. The paper shortage – due to the restriction of imports – compelled the newspapers to reduce their sheets to little more than pamphlets. Shops were compulsorily closed in the early evening. Yet complaints were rare. What were these petty deprivations compared with those our men experienced out yonder? At any rate, we could live – and live in comfort, too – for never was work more abundant, never were wages higher, never were the people at large in better circumstances.

And thus the story moves on to its appointed end. As we survey it, like a panorama that flashes before the eye, we see the dark days first – the casualty lists and the long columns of the noble dead. And what a record it is! Scarce a family seemed to have escaped. One Mayor of Doncaster lost two of his sons. An Alderman lost two, and was within an ace of losing a third. A councillor lost one. The Vicar of Doncaster lost one. Every Hall and Mansion knew the sound of mourning, as well as the humblest cottage. The very first casualty to reach the town was that of the son-in-law of Brigadier-General and Lady Bewicke Copley, of Sprotbrough Hall, the second was that bright young man, Lieutenant Campbell, who had been adopted as Parliamentary candidate for Doncaster, and left the town hurriedly on the very August Bank Holiday that war was declared – to die in less than a month in the Retreat from Mons. Nearly every country parsonage gave of its sons; and in every street in the town, in every village and hamlet, the sons of the people were numbered amongst the slain – all of them, rich and poor, high and low, dying side by side, and mingling their blood in the crimson earth that now covers their shattered forms. We calculate that in the Doncaster area alone, as revealed in the published casualty list, we lost over 5000 of our young manhood, and of these about 140 were officers.

On the other side, Doncaster had its full share of honours and decorations. Colonel Moxon, who commanded the 5th K.O.Y.L.I., received the C.M.G. Six V.C's came to the town and district. One of them went to Colonel Watson, who succeeded Colonel Moxon in the command of the 5th, and who was killed in action. Another went to a member of the Borough Police Force, P.C. Wyatt, a corporal in the Coldstream Guards; and another to Sergeant Calvert, a Conisborough lad, a soldier of the 5th. Two of these local heroes were adequately honoured by being entertained to complimentary banquets at the Mansion House by the then

Mayor. The D.S.O. was won by about twelve Doncaster Officers and, in addition, about 300 local soldiers or sailors received the Military Cross, or the Military Medal, or the Distinguished Conduct Medal; while there were others who received Italian, French, Belgian and Russian decorations. Among the recipients of Russian decorations was Mrs Balmforth, who received the Order of the Empress Alexandra for organising a Russian Flag Day during her period of office as Mayoress. Finally, the commandants and medical officers of the V.A.D. Hospitals, and the Chief of the Special Constables, received the insignia of the Order of the British Empire.

The town had its great days and its sad days – its intercession days and its solemn services at the Parish Church, the chief of which was that on the occasion of the death of Lord Kitchener. Few readers will remember yet the farewell when the Doncaster Engineers left the town on the completion of their period of training, and they will contrast those times with the mighty outburst of joy on Armistice Day. Since then there have been Peace Days, and moving services of praise at the Parish Church for the victory won; and we should not forget the dinners at the Mansion House to every returned soldier who had been a prisoner of war abroad, nor the great display when the 5th sent over from France for their Regimental Colours to be used on the triumphal march into Germany.

There were many things in Doncaster which once reminded us of the war. The Arnold Military Hospital, although closed, but the building, under the name St. George's Hospital, was latterly used for disabled and pensioned soldiers; and if the familiar 'blue uniform' of the wounded warrior was no longer to be seen in the streets, there was the daily spectacle of these ailing and shattered men walking slowly to St. George's for medical treatment. Our schools and public buildings reverted to their original uses. Every school in the town was claimed for the accommodation of troops, and it would have been a good thing if the corporation at the time could have placed a tablet in every school giving the names of the various regiments there billeted. It would impress the great fact of the war upon the mind of the rising generation in a manner not to be forgotten.

Outside the former site of Doncaster Museum at Beechfield, a tank, "Danum", stood as a grim reminder of the war. It was given to Doncaster by the government in recognition of the large amount of money raised in the town for the prosecution of the fight. Inside the museum is a monster steel shell, polished like silver and bearing an inscription. This was presented to the community for the same reason as the tank. The Cenotaph stands proudly on Bennetthorpe, at the gates of Elmfield Park and in the Mansion House a massive brass panel, given by Councillor Balmforth, who was Mayor during the two most strenuous years of the war, commemorates the Doncaster Division of Engineers, and gives the names of those of its members who died. A memorial somewhat similar is erected in the Parish Church to perpetuate the parishioners who gave their lives.

Chapter 17

Doncaster Floods

The joys and perils of living in the Don valley

By the year 1700 Marshgate was made up of just 4 houses.
The river Cheswold dissected a part of it and was said to be
'as nature had left it'. In 1735 there was an increase of 7
properties, and by the 1760s there was a considerable
increase in the number of properties there. Back then, much
the same as today, Marshgate was out on a limb. From the
recent floods which engulfed town end Bentley, parts of
Sprotbrough, together with Marshgate we can see that little
much has changed through the centuries regarding its
vulnerability given its close proximity to the main water
courses in town.

Hatfield writes, in his Historical Notices of Doncaster –
1868, "Now and then the accumulated waters have lain waste
the fairest lands and prostrated the works of man". He
recalls with vivid memories "the alarming disaster of
February 8th, 1861" where "the tide overflowed the banks of
the river with an irresistible force; and, as if impatient of
restraint, broke through bridges, snapped asunder gates and

palings, threw back the increasing streams from ancient drains and water courses, swept itself in solemn majesty over opposing obstacles, chafed, fretted, and roared through bridge and culvert, stopped water wheels and mill wheels, rushed into cellars of cottages, and crept upstairs to the house apartments, dashed through smaller tenements, out of the way nooks and corners, threw into utter confusion the occupiers of farm homesteads, disturbed beasts in their sheds, alarmed fowls on their perches, filled saw pits, and timber floated about like mere toys, deluged village lanes and byways, ever pressing onwards in its destructive career; at one fell swoop, game of all kinds, from the timid hare to the bright plumed pheasant were carried away regardless of the preserver; at length, tired and disappointed, the turbulent waters rolled backwards, and places hitherto free were turned upside down; but again returning with another violent effort to escape dashed forward, carrying death and terror in its path, until it found vent in the tidal waters of the Humber".

Lady Pitts Bridge was constructed by Joseph Lockwood and is a rather grand looking series of arches spanning over 100 yards. It would appear, to the untrained eye, to be a classic case of over-engineering on Lockwood's part, as the water it bridges is a mere ditch measuring about 3 feet wide. Do not be fooled! The trickle becomes a torrent in times of flood as the Don Navigation overflows at Crimpsall under (and sometimes over) the Sprotbrough road, behind the houses of

Northfield road and on towards Morrisons supermarket. On November 20th, 1791, Lady Pitts Bridge successfully resisted the pressure of such a torrent. Part of one of the arches was thrown to the ground but the bridge remained intact. On the low lands around it the waters settled at a depth of 6 feet allowing boats to sail across them with ease. The boats were used to ferry the milkmen, butchers, and bakers from house to house, making their deliveries through the upstairs windows. One Bentley farmer lost "three score of fine sheep" on that fateful day.

In a similar flood in the summer of 1828 the waters of the Cheswold rose rapidly on the morning of Sunday 13th July. Farm workers hurriedly attempted to rescue the hay in Crimpsall. A number of labourers were employed during the whole of that day, in "attempting to hinder the progress of the water, by raising the western bank from the foundry near the Mill Bridge to Newton. It continued to swell, and on Monday, the northern bank of the Mill Dyke gave way. The efforts to remedy this breach were fruitless; and the Ings of Bentley and Arksey became deluged". The area of Crimpsall where only 3 days before had seen the rescue of the hay, now became a boating marina for the pleasure seekers of the town.

The water in Crimpsall, as viewed from Friar's Bridge, presented one unbroken, glassy surface. "The reflections of the rays of the glorious sun, the forms of the ever varying clouds, the willows which fringed the southern side and the trees along the line of the Cheswold exhibited a novel spectacle".

The flood waters in French Gate reached the Brown Cow public house. "At one period of the flood a curious sight was observed in the shape of what appeared to be a floating island drifting slowly with the stream. The water careering along in its unopposed course swept with it, in one compact body, a huge mass of earth, flags, sedges, and rushes from the pool at Arksey, and the moving island had all the appearance of *terra firma* as it glided down the flood".
The problems that occurred time after time down in Marshgate were caused, mainly because of the Newton Bank which reinforced the river bank from what is now St Marys Bridge to the Hamlet of Newton itself. It was always the bank on the Marshgate side that the waters breached, forever causing much devastation there, until that is, the flood of Saturday 6th August, 1846. A decision was made to let the banks fail on the Newton side for a change. Hatfield writes, "The Newton Bank, the main cause of the mischief, was cut, at all hazards, opposite the south end of the Black Pond. From thence it ran across Sprotbrough road, past Anchorage Farm, made its way beneath Willow Bridge on the Great North Road, and joined the swollen brook stream of the Boiling Basin at Cusworth Ponds to the south side of Bentley Bank, and so on to the tide-way at Thwaite House. The relief afforded to Marshgate was apparent. Crimpsall had the

appearance of a large pool; and the long lines of light from the lamps at the Railway Station, and the public ones elsewhere, reflected from the scarcely rippled surface of the water, had a striking effect, while the distant roar of the river weir, and that of the rushing stream through the bank cutting, produced a picture rarely seen in this part of the country".

The men that were responsible for making the cut in Newton Bank did so without thought for their own safety. They also cared not for the consequences of such an act as; it was not their place to make such a decision. What was to be their fate?

"They were harassed and charged on the information of Benjamin Mangham, Lock Keeper, that they 'did, then and there, unlawfully, maliciously, and feloniously, break down, and cut down, a certain bank of a certain river, called the river Don, there situate, by means whereof certain lands were then and there overflowed and damaged, against the form of the statute in that case made and provided'. On Saturday August 28th, at the Town Hall, the case was heard before Richard Heber Wrightson, Esq. John William Sturges, Esq. Wm. Aldam, Esq. James Brown, Esq. Sir Isaac Morley, and Captain Bower, and occupied nine columns of the supplement to the Doncaster Gazette of Sept 1st".

To cut a long story short, the bench decided that no further action would be taken against the men on the grounds that, the corporation probably should have stepped in themselves but failed to do so, and in addition, the bank was more than likely erected illegally in the first place anyway. The case against the men was dismissed. It was later found that the bank had been constructed higher than the floors of the houses in Marshgate which speaks for itself really; the flood waters would reach the doorstep of the dwellings before it breached Newton Bank.

In June 2007, the waters of the Don once again rose and breached the Newton Bank at Black Pond. The water began to seek out all its ancient ways and dry stream beds came back to life. Ponds appeared where fields should be and rivers flowed where roads should be. The route that the waters took in the middle 19th century was the exact same route that they took in 2007. This highlights to me the fact, that we are guests on this earth, we can try to change nature, we can attempt to re-route water courses and build houses on seemingly safe tracts of land, however, when nature needs an escape route, the best engineers in the land cannot stand in its path.

Chapter 18

The Future - a prediction from the past

91 years ago in 1921 Ernest Phillips, the editor of the Doncaster Chronicle newspaper speculated on the future of the town. The following article is some of his predictions. Did he get it right? Let's see:

"Doncaster is ever changing. Unlike some old towns – Chester, Lancaster, and York – it retains none of its mediaeval characteristics. It is essentially modern. It has been built and rebuilt times without number. It is now undergoing its greatest change.

For centuries it was a quiet market town. There was no bustle and clang of commerce, no feverish race for wealth in industry. The smoke of Sheffield and the activity of Leeds seemed a long way off. At the beginning of the last century (early 1800), Doncaster was described as one of the handsomest residential towns in the whole of England. The massive houses of Hall Gate, Priory Place, and a few other thoroughfares testified that it was a town where well-to-do families loved to take life easily and placidly.

A change has now come over the scene. Doncaster is destined to be the centre of a great and rich industry. The base of this country's industrial greatness is coal. Wherever you find coal, there you find trade and industry active – iron and steel works, cotton and woollen mills, engineering shops, and the hundred and one manifestations of our national genius for making things.

There is coal all around Doncaster and, in fact, under Doncaster as well. There is coal under the race-course, there is coal under the corporation reservoir at Thrybergh. It stretches right to the East Coast, dipping deeper and deeper, until it reaches a depth where it is unworkable. But it is workable all around Doncaster, and this has led to a remarkable development during the last 15 years (since 1906). Over half a dozen new coal-pits have been sunk and are now working daily. The nearest to Doncaster is at Bentley, scarce 3 miles away. Others are at Carcroft, Askern, Woodlands, Edlington, Rossington, Hatfield, Thorne, etc., and others are in contemplation at Armthorpe, Finningly, and elsewhere.

As a direct result of this is that a network of villages are springing up around the town. A modern colliery gives employment to 2 or 3 thousand hands. It raises 2 or 3 thousand tons of coal each day. Some of them, like the one at Hickleton, only about 7 miles out of Doncaster, raise even 4,000 tons per day. A village springs up. It houses 5 or 6 thousand folk. A new church is erected, chapels and schools are reared, shops and picture-houses and clubs appear almost by magic; and lo, where a year ago you had a sleepy hamlet, now you have a throbbing industrial town, with a rattle of railway wagons, the clang of pit head gear, and all the usual features of town life.

These new centres look to Doncaster. They are linked up by means of the electric tram car. They come into town and do a great deal of their shopping which benefits financially everyone. One result already seen is the newly built shops which adorn our streets. Our theatres, our music halls, our public institutions, all benefit by these new populations which now cover what was once the sparsely populated countryside. But this is not all. Where there is coal there is other trade, and so we find that other industries are coming to Doncaster. Before the coal boom of the last few years, Doncaster could not be called a manufacturing town. True, there was the large establishment of the Great Northern Railway, where anything can be made from a handcart to an express locomotive; and, in addition, there were brass and wire works, etc.

But the working of the new coalfield will change, and is changing, all this. Just outside Doncaster, at Sandall, a mere hamlet on the river bank, a Lancashire glass-making firm built a factory to find work for 5,000 employees; they will construct a model village, with a church and club and library. Another Lancashire firm of woollen manufacturers are coming to Bentley, even nearer than Sandall, and they will build a large works for the manufacture of their own specialities. Further away, at Finningley, a Sheffield firm is building a vast place wherein to make motor cars.

In short, Doncaster is on the eve of a great development. At least half a dozen firms have come or are coming into the town. Others are making enquiries for land. The selection of Doncaster is due to several facts that give the town an advantage. It is not only on the main line of the Great Northern Railway, but 6 other railways have running power into Doncaster. Moreover, the canal which runs through Doncaster on its way from Sheffield to Goole and Hull, not only links us up with Sheffield, but gives us direct access to the sea. If this canal is widened and deepened, and made a real ship canal, as it almost certainly will be in the not too distant future, its value to the trade of the town will be greatly increased.

To make a modern manufacturing town, there are several essentials. The first and greatest is coal. Doncaster is not only the centre of the newest but the richest coalfield in Great Britain. It is true that it is a great depth. Some of the new pits are over 900 yards deep, more than half a mile; but modern engineering skill has overcome the difficulties of getting coal at that enormous depth. Powerful fans drive fresh air from above down one shaft, and after it has circulated through all the galleries it is sucked up another shaft. Engines nowadays can be made strong enough to draw coal to the bank from almost any depth.

Thus the manufacturer has plenty of coal at Doncaster. The coal merchant has seven railways and a canal at his service if he wants to sell it or ship it to a country across the sea. Doncaster, therefore, is in a good position to make headway; and while some enthusiasts think the town may someday be a second Leeds or Sheffield, there are others who think its greatest developments will be its coal trade, and that it may be in a few years time a second Cardiff as a coal distributing centre.

These things, however, are in the future. How soon they may be upon us, none may say; but that the town is changing every day is a certainty. Within the last 12 years nearly ten new pits have been opened; half a dozen new branch railway lines have been constructed; at least three or more model villages have been planned; four or five new churches have been erected and consecrated. Tramway lines have been extended from the town to three colliery villages, and the Corporation has projects for others.

The probability is that Doncaster in a generation will have completely changed its character. Its rural aspect will have gone. It will be a busy manufacturing town. A ring of coal mines will encircle it. Iron works, glass works, woollen mills, engineering shops will stand where now the farmhand drives his team and the ploughshare furrows the loam. The canal will bear on its bosom the products of mine and mill on their way to coastal ports for shipment over the seas.

The town itself will change. The last remnants of old Doncaster – in such narrow thoroughfares as Scot Lane – will disappear. Broad streets will be the rule. The tramcars will link up with every outside centre of life and trade. There will be little left to remind the visitor that he stands within one of the oldest boroughs of England – a town of Roman foundation, a borough that has lived its life in all the succeeding ages of Saxon and Dane and Norman lordship; that has echoed to the tramp of Roman Legions; that has seen Saxon and Norman at deadly grips; that has emerged out of feudal darkness into the fierce white light of 20th century civilization.

It is in order that the story of the coloured pageant of our past may be imprinted on the mind of young Doncaster that this [piece] is written – that in regarding the present and speculating about the future, we may not be unmindful of a past which comes down to us as a very precious heritage.

Chapter 19

Doncaster Today - as of 1960

General Information

- Population – 84,610
- Area – 8,371 acres
- Rateable value – £1,275,280
- Rates in the £ – 22s 6d
- Number of houses and flats in corporation schemes – 8,836

In the middle of the last century the face of Doncaster began to change, for the coming of the railway in 1848, followed by the former Great Northern Railway plant and carriage works in 1853, transformed an agricultural and market town to a semi-industrial one. Other industries soon followed and, later, coal-pits,- amongst the finest for production in the world – began to be sunk in the immediate neighbourhood. By the 1914-18 war the South Yorkshire coalfield was well established and today Doncaster is surrounded by large mining villages, some of which are set out in the best town-planning standards. Some adjoin the County Borough, and those of Armthorpe, Edlington and Rossington, the now industrialised Barnby-Dun-with-Kirk-Sandall, with the Urban Districts of Adwick-le-street and Bentley-with-Arksey, help to bring the population within ten miles of the town centre to approximately 320,000.

The shopping and business potential of the town is therefore apparent. For shops and stores Doncaster can compare with many of its larger neighbours, and its markets are noted throughout the North.

The quick growth of the town since the early part of the century is partly due to this and also to the fact that in 1923 the Corporation inaugurated an industrial development scheme which has attracted various new industries. This scheme provided land for factories adjacent to the then Sheffield and South Yorkshire Navigation Company's waterway, with road and railway adjoining, and has enabled these industries to be established and operated on the edge of the town in pleasant surroundings. The variety of manufacturers together with the nearby coalfields, combine to make Doncaster one of the most prosperous towns in the North of England. For the last century the town has been noted for its confectionary and it is still a thriving industry.

The Corporation has played a big part in this development, and street improvements, schools, colleges, housing, water, gas and electricity, together with open spaces, recreation grounds, hospitals, health services and clinics, with other services necessary to the well-being of the community, have been provided in full measure.

In November, 1959, St. Mary's Bridge was opened and named by H.R.H. the Princess Royal. This new bridge forms the northern exit from the County Borough, and replaces a bridge opened in 1899. Former bridges were known as the Mill Bridge, on account of the former Corporation water-driven manorial Corn Mills immediately adjacent, but there is evidence that stone bridges had existed from Norman times. The road approaching was known in olden times as St. Mary's Gate and on the mediaeval bridge there was a Chantry Chapel dedicated to the Virgin Mary, from which the bridge was known.

In education much progress has been made and many developments have taken place since the war. The ever-increasing school population has necessitated the building of many new schools and older schools have been adapted to modern requirements. The new housing estates have primary and secondary schools. Playing fields are provided with these new schools, and for the benefit of the older schools there are extensive playing fields situated near the centre of the town. There is still a substantial schools building programme ahead, the quality of which will rank with the best in the country.

The Grammar School, founded in the 14th century, is at present housed in a building designed by Sir Gilbert Scott in 1864; in 1938 considerable additions were made. The school has a fine hall, swimming baths and adjoining playing fields. The old school hall is now used as the school library.

The High School for Girls is situated near the new Civic Centre.

There are two Technical High Schools, one for girls, and one for boys in excellent premises.

A Special School for educationally sub-normal children has been established at Rossington Hall, six miles south of the town.

The Doncaster Technical College, at present situated in St. George Gate, is being replaced over a number of years by new buildings at the Civic Centre site in Waterdale. The new buildings now provide for the Electrical Engineering, Building and Pure Science, Household Science, Commerce and Music departments. There are over 6000 students and classes, in addition to those departments already mentioned, in Mechanical Engineering, Automobile Engineering, Mining, Modern Languages, Drama, Works Management, Trade Courses and preparation for University examinations.

The School of Art has approximately 500 students and will, in time, be replaced by new buildings. The present school is situated in Dockin Hill Road.

Part time activities are catered for in evening institutes, Education Centres, Community Centres, and Youth Clubs. The

Youth Employment Service is available for advice and information for young people up to the age of 18.

A Training College for Teachers has been established at High Melton Hall near Doncaster; where there are at present 215 students. The College will be further extended.

The Arts Centre, maintained by the Education Committee, caters for Drama and Films.

The Central Public Library in St. George Gate was erected in 1889 in commemoration of Queen Victoria's Jubilee. It comprises Lending and Reference Libraries, Reading Rooms, and a separate Children's Library. Branch Libraries are situated at Balby (High Road), Wheatley (Parkway South), Intake (Community Centre), Hexthorpe (Community Centre), Cantley (Everingham Road), and Bessacarr (Infants' School). There is also a Schools Libraries Service supplying books to upwards of 40 school departments. Membership of the Yorkshire Regional Library System, in which the Libraries act as a sub-zonal centre, places the Library resources of the whole country at the service of the student and the specialist reader.

At the Museum and Art Gallery, Waterdale, works of art are displayed in the local collection, and from time to time exhibitions of paintings, sculptures, etchings, and photographs from other collections and from local societies are held. In the

Museum there are many exhibits well worth inspection. The history of the town and neighbourhood is set out from prehistoric times and the Roman collection is particularly strong. A comprehensive collection of birds, mammals, and insects, particularly local, is shown. A miniature Zoo in connection with the Museum was established in 1955. Plans are now completed for a projected new Museum and Art Gallery, which is scheduled to start this year (1960). The former delightful gardens and grotto behind the Museum have now disappeared to make way for the new College of Further Education.

Reference has already been made to Doncaster's Markets, which are amongst the largest and finest in the country. There is a Market Hall with up to date shops and stands, a covered Fish and General market, a large covered miscellaneous and dry-goods market, an open market with its colourful stalls, and a Cattle Market. The Cattle Market is being reconstructed on the adjoining Dockin Hill and new sheep, pig, and poultry markets have been opened. On completion, the livestock markets will be the most up-to-date in the country. In addition, there is a Corn Exchange, one of the town's largest buildings, which was erected in 1873, and is still used on Saturdays for its original purpose. It is also the venue for boxing, wrestling, and other sporting events, and for concerts and meetings. During the day it is used as a Municipal Restaurant. The Abattoirs, Meat Stores, and Cold Stores are also part of the market undertaking. There are Pleasure Fairs at various times of the year, the chief one being during September Race Week.

Market days are on Tuesdays, Fridays, and Saturdays, and large crowds of shoppers are drawn into the town on these days from the suburbs and surrounding districts.

Doncaster is fortunate in its Parks and Open Spaces, which are being added to from time to time. The principal Parks and Gardens are:

- Elmfield Park – of 23 acres comprising rose gardens, bowling greens (3), putting green, hard tennis courts (8), floral features, and children's playground.
- Westfield Park – in which there are bowling greens (2), hard tennis courts (3), putting green, and children's playground.
- Sandall Park – of 53 acres, with a cafe, boating lake, golf course (9 hole), putting green, football pitches (4), children's playground, and a car park.
- Grove Gardens – a delightful little park with bowling and putting greens and two hard tennis courts.
- Hexthorpe Flatts – a popular resort of 28 acres, in which is situated The Dell, a well known beauty spot, with band-stand, bowling greens (2), hard tennis courts (6), putting green, and children's playground.

- Cantley Park – now in course of development, which will provide ample recreation facilities for the Cantley neighbourhood unit.
- Haslam Park – a small park at Bessacarr, which includes a bowling green, hard tennis courts, and children's playground.
- Sandall Beat Wood Playing Fields – with ten football pitches, three hockey pitches, and three cricket squares, with modern pavilion accommodation.

There are also numerous ornamental gardens maintained by the Corporation in various parts of the town, including Regent Square, whilst other open spaces include Sandall Beat Wood, the Race Common, and the Town Fields.

As a result of the rapid growth of the town, housing became the first importance and the number of houses erected by the Corporation placed the town well in the forefront of the whole of the country. Since the end of the war, in 1946, nearly 5000 houses and flats have been constructed, bringing the total number owned by the Corporation to approximately 8900. There are large, well-laid-out estates at Intake, Weston Road, Woodfield, Warmsworth Road, Wheatley Park, Clay Lane, and Cantley; the latter estate, when fully completed, will be the largest with 3200 houses. Transport services, shopping centres, with community centres and schools have already been provided and in some cases existing woodland have been incorporated in the lay-out. The Corporation have also provided land for private builders, the Hills Lane Estate being a recent example of this co-operation.

Municipal Departments

- Town Clerk's Office – 1 Priory Place (Tel. 4051)
- Borough Treasurer's Office (including rates and local taxation office) – (53-54 Hall Gate (Tel. 4041)
- Borough Surveyor's Office (Including works dept.) – 2 Priory Place (Tel. 4051)
- Town Planning Department – Pells Close (Tel. 4051)
- Allotments Department – Old Exchange Brewery, Cleveland Street (Tel. 4051)
- Building Inspector's Office – Old Exchange Brewery, Cleveland Street (Tel. 4051)
- Borough Architect's Office – 15 South Parade (Tel. 2404)
- Housing Manager – 15 South Parade (Tel. 2404)
- Medical Officer of Health – Wood Street (Tel. 2447)
- Chief Public Health Inspector – Wood Street (Tel. 2447)
- Chief Education Officer – Whitaker Street (Tel. 49211)
- Police Department – The Guildhall, Frenchgate (Tel. 2222)
- Transport Department – Leicester Avenue (Tel. 2451)
- Race Manager – Grandstand, Racecourse (Tel. 2706)
- Fire Service – Lonsdale Avenue (Tel. 4468)
- Museum and Art Gallery – Beechfield, Waterdale (Tel. 2095)
- Public Library – St. George Gate (Tel. 2676)
- Markets Department – Cattle Market (Tel. 2796)

- Municipal Restaurant – Corn Exchange, Market Place (Tel. 3364)
- Weights and Measures Office – 78 Frenchgate (Tel. 2680)
- Civic Welfare Office – Wood Street (Tel. 3589)
- Children's Department – Wood Street (Tel. 4806)
- Parks Department – Elmfield Park (Tel. 2807)
- Cemeteries and Crematorium Superintendent – Rose Hill Cemetery (Tel. 55191)
- Superintendent Registrar (Births, Deaths, and Marriages) – 1 Priory Place (Tel. 4051)
- Registrars of Births, Deaths, and Marriages – Factory Lane (Tel. 61439)
- Civil Defence Officer – Cleveland Street (Tel. 49952)
- Baths Superintendent – St. James' Street Baths (Tel. 3000)
- Water Department – Sandy Lane

Ambulance Station – Armthorpe Road

Assistance Board – Hall Gate

Banks:

- Barclays – 3 High Street, 155 Balby Road, and Hall Gate
- Co-operative Wholesale Bankers Ltd. – 7 Station Road
- Lloyds – High Street
- Martins – 21 Baxter Gate
- Midland – High Street
- National Provincial – 47 High Street

- Westminster – 12 High Street
- Williams Deacon's – 15 St. Sepulchre Gate
- York County Savings Bank – 50 Hall Gate, 80 High Road Balby, and 247 Beckett Road
- Yorkshire Penny – 16 High Street

Baths:

- Grey Friars Road
- St. James' Street

Bowling Green's:

- Elmfield Park
- Hexthorpe Flatts
- Grove Gardens
- Haslam Park
- Westfield Park

Cemeteries:

- Doncaster – Carr House Road
- Rose Hill – Cantley Lane
- Crematorium – Rose Hill, Cantley Lane

Chamber of Commerce – Miss A. Parkinson, Secretary, Dolphin Chambers, 44a Market Place.

Citizens Advice Bureau and Council of Social Service – 13 Thorne Road

Cinemas:

- Astra – Beckett Road
- Essoldo – Silver Street
- Gaumont – Hall Gate
- Odeon – Hall Gate
- Picture House – High Street
- Windsor – Warmsworth Road

County Council Divisional Offices – Station Road

County Court – St. James' Street

Cricket – Doncaster Town C.C. and many other Works and Private clubs

Customs and Excise – 27 Silver Street

Dance and Ballrooms:

- St. James' Baths Hall
- Corn Exchange
- Co-operative Emporium
- Berry's – Printing Office Street
- Bullar's – 104 St. Sepulchre Gate
- also Hotel Ballrooms

Early Closing – Thursdays

Education Offices – Whitaker Street

Electricity:

- Doncaster Service Centre – 20 Hall Gate
- Number 5 Sub Area – District Office, 24 Thorne Road
- Power Station – Crimpsall

Employment Exchange – Factory Lane

Fire Brigade – Lonsdale Avenue (Tel. 4468)

Football:

- (Soccer) Doncaster Rovers FC – Belle Vue Ground
- (Soccer) Doncaster United FC – Airport Ground (amateur)
- (Rugby) Doncaster R.U.F.C. – Armthorpe Road Ground
- (Rugby League) Doncaster R.L.F.C. – Bentley Road Ground

Gas:

- Works – Dockin Hill Road
- Showrooms and Enquiry Offices – Silver Street

Gliding Club – Airport

Golf Clubs:

- Doncaster – Bessacarr
- Wheatley – Armthorpe Road

- Town Moor – Race Course

Health Executive Council – 39 Market Place

Hospitals:

- Royal Infirmary – Thorne Road
- Western Hospital – Springwell Lane
- Infectious Diseases – Tickhill Road
- St. Catherine's – Tickhill Road
- (See also Maternity Homes)

Hotels – Among the Principals are:

- Danum – High Street
- Elephant – St. Sepulchre Gate
- Punch's – Bawtry Road
- Earl of Doncaster Arms – Bennetthorpe
- Rockingham – Bennetthorpe
- Woolpack – Market Place
- Angel and Royal – Frenchgate (all above are licensed)
- St. Margaret's – Christ Church Terrace
- Waverley – 9 St. George Gate
- Regent – Regent Square
- Auckland – 4 Auckland Road
- Springfield – 1 Albion Place (Private)

Housing Department – 15 South Parade

Library (Public) – St. George Gate

Magistrate's Clerk – The Guildhall

Maternity Homes:

- Hamilton Lodge – Carr House Road
- Hamilton Annexe – Springwell Lane
- Fairfield – 91 Thorne Road (Private)

Ministry of National Insurance – Kingsway House, Hall Gate

Museum and Art Gallery – Beechfield, Waterdale

Newspapers:

- Doncaster Chronicle – Scot Lane
- Doncaster Gazette – Printing Office Street
- Doncaster Free Press – Sunny Bar (weekly on Thursdays)
- Yorkshire Evening Post – Scot Lane
- Yorkshire Evening News – Printing Office Street (evening)
- Sheffield Telegraph – West Laith Gate (daily)
- Yorkshire Post – Scot Lane (daily)

Omnibus Stations:

- Glasgow Paddocks – Waterdale
- Christ Church
- Marshgate
- Station Yard
- North Bridge

- Trafford Street

Parking Places:

- Market Place
- Dockin Hill
- Duke Street
- Trafford Street
- High Fishergate
- Princes Street
- Waterdale
- Factory Lane
- Lord Street
- and many private streets and roads

Police:

- County Borough – The Guildhall
- West Riding – 35 West Laith Gate

Playing Fields – Town Field

Post Office – Priory Place

Putting Greens:

- Elmfield Park
- Grove Gardens
- Sandall Park
- Hexthorpe Flatts

- Westfield Park

Rotary Club – Earl of Doncaster Arms Hotel (Mondays 1pm)

Rural District Council Offices – Netherhall Road

Restaurants and Cafes – among the principals are:

- Chambers' – 43 Waterdale
- Coopland's – Hall Gate and Silver Street
- A. Davy and Sons Ltd. – 37-39 Frenchgate
- Costa Brava – Hall Gate
- Ye Olde Barrel – 50-52 Frenchgate
- Grill Room – 30 Hall Gate
- Hodgson & Hepworth Ltd. – St. Sepulchre Gate
- Municipal – Corn Exchange
- Odeon – Hall Gate
- Gaumont – Hall Gate
- Carlton – Sunny Bar
- Doncaster Co-operative – The Emporium, St. Sepulchre Gate
- Priestnall's – Station Road
- Fisher's – 16 Wood Street
- Elvin's – 13 Hall Gate
- Jons – Priory Place
- Golden Phoenix – Cleveland Street

Theatres:

- Arts Centre – Waterdale

- Gaumont – Hall Gate

Tennis Courts (Public):

- Elmfield Park
- Grove Gardens
- Haslam Park
- Hexthorpe Flatts
- Westfield Park

Worship, Places of:

- Church of England

- St. John's – Balby
- St. Wilfrid's – Cantley
- Christ Church – Thorne Road
- St. George's – St. George Gate
- St. James' – St. Sepulchre Gate
- St. Jude's – Hexthorpe
- St. Mary's – Beckett Road
- St. Aiden's – Wheatley Hills
- All Saints – Intake Estate
- St. Paul's – Parkway North
- St. Peter's – Warmsworth Road
- St. Hugh of Lincoln – Cantley Estate

- Methodist

- Methodist Chapel – Printing Office Street

- Balby Road Methodist Chapel
- Oxford Place Methodist Chapel
- Methodist Chapel – Carr House Road
- Methodist Church – Urban Road
- Methodist Church – Nether Hall Road
- Methodist Church – Highfield Road
- Urban Road Methodist Church
- Methodist Church Beckett Road
- Methodist Chapel – Alder Grove
- Methodist Church – Goodison Boulevard

- Roman Catholic

- St. Peter's – Princes Street
- Church of the Sacred Heart – Warmsworth Road
- Our Lady of Mount Carmel and St. Mary Magdalene – Armthorpe Road
- St. Paul's – Goodison Boulevard

- Other denominations

- Trinity Presbyterian Church – Waterdale
- Friends' Meeting House – West Laith Gate
- Baptist Chapel – Chequer Road
- Wheatley Park Baptist Church – Winchester Avenue
- Congregational Church – Hall Gate
- Intake Congregational Church – Ardeen Road
- Christians' Meeting House – The Holmes
- Providence Meeting House – Spring Gardens

- Villa Park Hall Plymouth Brethren – Cantley Estate
- Free Christian Church – Hall Gate
- National Progressive Spiritualist Church – Catherine Street
- National Spiritualist Church – Baker Street
- Plymouth Brethren – 48 Becket Road
- Pentecostal Hall – Portland Place
- Salvation Army Citadel – Trafford Street
- Gospel Hall – Carr House Road
- Welcome Mission Hall – Baker Street
- Welsh Congregational Chapel – South Parade
- Latter Day Saints – 1 Auckland Road
- Synagogue – Canterbury Road
- Jehovah's Witnesses – 44 Market Place
- Salvation Army Hall – Lonsdale Avenue
- First Church of Christ Scientist – 98 Balby Road
- Flintwood Methodist Church – Marlowe Road, Intake

Y.W.C.A. – Cleveland Street

Y.M.C.A. – St. Sepulchre Gate

Prehistoric Doncaster would have looked like this

Peat Bogs at Thorne Moors

Doncaster, High Street

Hall-Gate, Doncaster   Published by T. W. Draper, Doncaster

284 YORK ROAD AND BARNSLEY ROAD
DONCASTER.

© Doncaster History Publishing 2012

www.doncasterhistory.co.uk

DONCASTER HISTORY

2536652R00110

Printed in Great Britain
by Amazon.co.uk, Ltd.,
Marston Gate.